P9-DTC-959

BUZZ FOR *BUZZING COMMUNITIES*

"Richard Millington has long been one of my go-tos when I need advice that is actionable, concise and—perhaps most importantly—easily explainable to stakeholders. *Buzzing Communities* is a fantastic compilation of some of the best of that knowledge. I wish I'd had this reference when I started out but even now, after almost a decade of managing communities, I found nuggets of wisdom and a strategic approach to community building that has helped me explain and implement the what, the why and the how more effectively and with fewer hiccups. If you want a road map for building a strong and successful community, this is it."

—Justin Isaf, Director of Communities, Huffington Post

"Richard Millington's book is a rocket up the backside of any community manager, however experienced. As you read it, it dawns on you that community management is an evolving field and, for that reason, there's constantly more you could do to enhance your community. Whether it's optimising your registration process, tweaking the tone of your emails or illustrating the return on investment of your work, Millington has it covered.

Unlike other community management books, he's not all theory and no trousers; there are practical tips for everything from checking the source code to see what platform a community uses to how to conduct a psychographic interview. All in all, Millington has written a comprehensive and time-saving step-by-step handbook which feels like he's telling you something very valuable while leaving you some room to formulate your own ideas."

—Ben Whitelaw, Communities Editor, The Times

"All I needed to know about building a community powered with passion and making it bubble with activity. A must read."

—Vanessa Von Vanessar, GreenPeace

Yes, you can "manage" an online community without losing the human touch. This book provides practical ideas to help you understand the health and development of your online community, based on Millington's repeated experience, not merely anecdotes. It includes guidance on which metrics to track (and which ones *not* to track), as well as on balancing your management activities, depending on the life cycle stage of the community. Both new and experienced community managers will find helpful advice, whether they're starting a new community, or taking responsibility for an existing one.

—Janet Swisher, Developer, Mozilla

Buzzing Communities

How To Build Bigger, Better, and More
Active Online Communities

BY RICHARD MILLINGTON

Acknowledgments

I never thought I would write a book. That I did is a testament to all the people who have helped me throughout the years.

Special thanks to Angie Petkovic and Henry Warren for having a bigger impact on my life and career than they realize.

Further thanks to all the people I've worked with, especially Matt Cheney, Helen Lynch, and Judi Huck.

Also thanks to continuous sources of inspiration from Seth Godin, Blaise Grimes-Viort, Justin Isaf, Kirsten Wagenaar, Alison Michalk, Venessa Paech, Ramit Sethi, Patrick O'Keefe (make sure you read his book too!), Martin Reed, Rachel Happe, Jim Storer, Jono Bacon, Jake McKee, Philip Wride, David McMillan, David Chavis, Cliff Lampe, Brian Butler, Erik Johnston, Sue John, Tamara Littleton, Tia Fisher and everyone else working in community management.

A huge thank you to Robin Dellabough for putting up with me and helping create a book I'm proud to have (finally) written.

Finally, a special thank you to my wife, Skirmante Millington . . . for everything.

Copyright © Richard Millington 2012. All rights reserved.

No part of this book may be used or reproduced by any means, graphic, electronic, or mechanical, including photocopying, recording, or by any information storage retrieval system without the written permission of the author except in the case of brief quotations embodied in critical articles and reviews.

ISBN: 978-0-9883599-0-1

Contents

Introduction

How is your community doing?

This is a simple question.

Your answer will probably be quite short: My community is fine.

You might well be right, so let's ask something a little more specific.

Is your community doing better than last month? Is your community healthier? Are members more engaged? Are members happier? Has the Return On Investment (ROI) of your community increased? Has your community grown? Do members feel a stronger sense of community?

How many of these questions can you answer?

Or, more to the point, how many of your answers could you support with *data*? Can you *prove* that your answers are right?

Now, let's make this a little tougher: how are *you* doing as a community manager?

Can you prove you have increased the ROI of the community since you joined? Can you prove that you've grown membership, gotten members more engaged, boosted the sense of community? Can you prove you're a valuable asset instead of a wasteful expense?

These basic questions about you and your community will influence what you should work on next, whether your actions the previous month succeeded, whether you should be paid more (or less), and whether you should even have the job.

If you can't answer these questions with supporting data, you need to read this book.

Two amazing things about data

The first amazing thing about data is how much data there is right now. You can collect data on everything from a member's thoughts and feelings to how changing the color, font or copy on the platform can improve the registration process.

The second amazing thing is how little data we currently use. In 2009, my company, FeverBee, ran a survey among new clients asking them how they used data. Just fewer than 20% had a clear process for regularly collecting data, only 10% bothered to analyze data, and only one organization had a process for using the results of that analysis to influence future actions.

That's insane!

Data is the single best asset you have to develop a thriving community. You can use data to optimize every facet of the community management role. You can use data to become far more effective community managers than you are today.

But you need to use it correctly. You need to know what data to collect, how to collect it, how to analyze it, and how to use that data to identify future actions you should take.

Why we need our data

I was fired from my first ever community management job. I was 15 years old and delighted to be doing my dream job: running an online community about video gaming. I worked from home, in my own hours, earning close to a full-time salary. For a 15-year-old, that's not a bad gig.

I followed my job description to the letter. I did everything I had been told to do. I wrote content, responded to members, organized events/activities, resolved conflicts, and even learned how to optimize elements of the platform.

The problem was I had no idea if what I was doing benefited the organization I worked for. It was no big deal; I left the money side to the money men. That was their problem. So long as I followed my job description to the letter, I was fine.

You already know how this ends...

One morning I received a courtesy call that my position was being cut. It wasn't that I wasn't doing the job I had been hired for, I just couldn't prove that I had done a good job—nor that doing a good job profited the organization. I hadn't bothered to benchmark the community when I joined. I hadn't bothered to ascertain the metrics of growth, engagement, sense of community, nor ROI.

I didn't realize that my job description was simply a collection of all the things I *could* be doing. Not all the things I *should* be doing. As a result, I had been entirely reactive. I *reacted* to what happened in the community. Nothing I had done had improved the community in the long term.

Had growth increased? Were members more engaged? Was the community generating an increased ROI since I joined?

Who knew?

I tell you this story because the way I worked back then is the way many community managers are today. They're certainly not as naïve as I was back then, but they are still too reactive, too ad hoc, and too lacking in long-term strategy. They still fail to use their data!

Online community management is a role that's moving from the amateur wilderness into the professional mainstream. We need to get professional about it. Not a single community manager I've spoken with who has lost a job recently can tell me what his own ROI was. They can't tell me if they improved their community—or not.

We urgently need to change this lack of accountability. Many community managers are working for peanuts yet delivering incredible value. Some, like The Huffington Post's Justin Isaf, put metrics behind every action they take to show a quanti-fied ROI and savings.

But the goal of this book isn't about pay rises or job security (though data can help you with both). The goal is to transform your approach to community management and to convert good community managers into professionals. The goal is to introduce science into what we do. Professionals know the science. They know how to use data and proven theory.

We need to embrace data as the foundation for commu-nity management activities for several reasons. But how do you learn to do that?

In this guide I explain why you need to master your data, how to master your data, the proven social science theories that underpin your work and the simple steps to becoming a much better community manager.

I'm not going to lie—I am quite technical in places. I dis-cuss stratified sampling, thematic analysis, applied statistics, and other slightly scary sounding terms. There is no way to avoid this. You need to know the techniques of collecting and analyzing the right data.

Unlike trying to grasp the Lithium Community Health In-dex formula (below), however, you will be able to understand, step by step, what you need to do to collect, analyze and apply data to your community development efforts.

$$\chi = C_s \cdot \left\{ \text{signlog} \left(\left[\langle \frac{e^{-|t_o-t|/50}}{50} |dH_o(t)/dt - \langle dH_o(t)/dt \rangle_t |\rangle_t \right]^{-1/2} \right. \right.$$
$$\left. \left. \cdot \int_{-\infty}^{t_o} \frac{dH(t)}{dt} \frac{e^{-|t_o-t|/50}}{50} \, dt \right) + C_o \right\},$$

Lithium Community Health Index

(sorry Joe!)

The unseen

This happens a lot. A client approached us with a problem: *Members are fighting too often, help!*

This is a "seen" issue. It's highly visible. They think that it's causing a big problem within the community, and they want members to all get along.

But this assumption is entirely data-free. Members fighting with each other usually increase the amount of activity on the community platform. People keep returning to defend their point, or argue the ideas of others.

Fighting among members only becomes a problem when it spills into other categories/threads and prevents any other discussions from taking place. But, unless you're tracking your data, you will never know this. All you will see are the conflicts and be determined to take action.

Typically in this situation we begin tracking data and discover one of several things:

1. Fighting has had no impact on the visiting habits of anyone on the site.

2. Fighting has increased the amount of activity on the site.

3. There are far bigger problems to worry about.

The bigger problems are what we focus on. It's the invisible—unseen—problems that hurt the community most. The client in question had a one in 1,000 conversion ratio: for every 1,000 members who clicked the registration link to join the site, only one was still a regular member six months later.

This is what the client should be worried about. Without data this was an *unseen* problem. With data, you can spot the issue easily. With data you can use proven social science to design interventions to resolve this problem. With data you can track changes over time. But too many community managers aren't even using the basic elements of data at the moment.

The number of unseen problems is *HUGE!* When the number of new visitors to the platform dips, that's an unseen problem. When a number of regulars vanish, that's an unseen problem. When the volunteers begin slipping away, that's an unseen problem. When the number of responses to a typical discussion drops, that's an unseen problem. When a smaller and smaller number of members are contributing to an ever-greater percentage of discussions, that's an unseen problem.

Every one of these problems can potentially kill a community. Without an intervention, the community will slip into a decline, which is very difficult to reverse.

Vocal minorities and the time they steal

If you don't collect data, you're probably reacting solely to the vocal minority in your community. Different people have different personalities. A percentage of these people will regularly voice their opinions on your community efforts. They might be critical of a decision you've taken, a change in the platform, the way you resolved a conflict, and so forth.

You can waste a lot of time catering to the whims of this vocal minority without realizing that it's just a vocal minority. It's only those who are upset that typically voice their opinion. The happy members rarely state how happy they are about the current state of their community.

Unless you're collecting data, you won't know if the comments of the vocal minority carry any weight. You won't know if it reflects the silent majority. Typically, your data will show that the decisions you've made, the tweaks you've implemented, or the way you resolved a conflict have had little to no impact upon the level of activity in the community (or that you've improved the community). This means that the feelings of the majority haven't changed.

Therefore, you don't need to spend much time catering to the whims of the vocal minority. Yet, that's exactly what most community managers do. When the vocal minority speaks, they halt all plans and work on tasks that affect relatively few members.

A typical example: recently a community manager mentioned that she had spent half the day dealing with one community member. The member was upset that other members of the community had been subtly advertising their own products via their signature (and the community had recently allowed people to purchase advertising space on the platform).

Think about that for a moment. That's half a day on an activity that will only impact one member over the short-term. What happens when that member gets upset again—is that another half a day gone? What happens if two members get upset?

God forbid, what happens when 10 members a week get upset? That's all of your time spent trying to make chronically disgruntled members *slightly* happier. It's tempting to spend too much time making unhappy members happy instead of keeping the happy members happy.

How would a data-savvy community manager tackle this?

Data driven community managers know specifically what they have to achieve each day to further develop the community. They allocate their daily time. They make sure they tackle the long-term, high-impact tasks first. After that, they resolve member disputes and complaints. If they don't get through all the complaints/disputes within the time they set themselves, too bad—but at least they got the important work done.

What's a better use of your time, responding yet again to a disgruntled member or organizing an event members will be excited about? What is most likely to increase growth, engagement and develop a stronger sense of community? It's not even close.

Sure, responding to member complaints is important, but give it the low priority it deserves in the grand scheme of things.

In the dark

If you are a typical community manager, sometimes what you do just happens to work. Sometimes it doesn't. You simply have no way of knowing.

So you keep doing what you think *might* work—random, reactive activities—and hope that the community *feels* successful. You might keep repeating things that don't work indefinitely *and never even know it.*

Without mastering data, you're simply working in the dark. Without data, you're not a professional. Without data, you will never become better than you are right now. You can't optimize your activities. You can't proactively develop your community.

These are just a few examples that highlight the current nature of community management. If we properly use data, all of these problems are entirely fixable. So let's start shining the light of science on our community management.

## PART ONE

How to Manage Your Community

Before I explain how to optimize each element of community management, you need to understand the conceptual framework.

The role of the community manager can be broken into eight distinct elements: the community management framework. It's a template you can use for managing an online community.

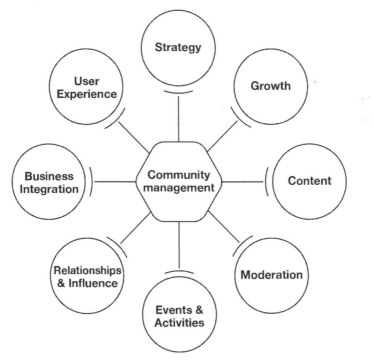

COMMUNITY MANAGEMENT ACTIVITIES

1. **Strategy.** Establishing and executing the strategy for developing the community.

2. **Growth.** Increase membership of the community and convert newcomers into regulars.

3. **Content.** Create, edit, facilitate, and solicit content for the community.

4. **Moderation.** Remove obstacles to participation and encourage members to make contributions.

5. **Events and activities.** Create and facilitate events to keep members engaged.

6. **Relationship and influence.** Build relationships with key members and gain influence within the community.

7. **Business integration.** Advocate internally within the organization and integrate business processes with community efforts.

8. **User experience.** Improve the community platform and participation experience for members.

The amount of time you spend on each component will vary, of course. To use a simple example, in the early stages of the community lifecycle, more time might be spent on growth and less time on business integration. As the community matures, you might spend more time on the user experience.

Generally speaking, the more mature the community, the more time you spend on macro-level activities that affect as many members as possible.

Each of these elements has a goal that benefits the development of the community. Each of these elements can be quantified with numerical data to measure the success of the effort. You can use proven data and theory to optimize each of these elements.

Optimizing all elements of this framework is the goal of part one of this book. I'm going to explain the theory behind each element and the data to optimize what you do.

## CHAPTER 1

Strategy

How will your community be better next week than it is now? When you went to work this morning, did you have a clear plan for what you were going to achieve today? Or did you react to what you saw in the community?

One of our first tasks with a new client is to ask the community manager to track his or her time. We've found that most community managers spend the majority of their time *reacting* to what happens in the community.

Most community managers don't have a strategic goal to achieve. They go to work each morning, see what happens in the community, and react to it. One community manager mentioned the workload was much easier now that her community was less active!

As a result they maintain their communities, but don't develop them. Do you have a strategy for your community right now? When you go to work, do you have a clear idea of what you're trying to achieve and how it fits in with the overall development of the community?

Strategy is, by far, the most important and most high-value work. People who strategize well combine profound understanding of community development with advanced project management skills. They're rare and invaluable.

However, though many community managers proclaim their strategic brilliance, few have a track record of successfully executing strategy. The vast majority of strategies lack two key elements: data and theory.

Most strategy efforts begin with the objective. What does the community need to achieve for the organization? They then create a plan to get there. That sounds logical but it ignores where you are now (data), what your audience wants (audience analysis), and how communities develop (theory). Many strategies are also rigid, failing to change regardless of what else happens in the community.

You get the benefits you want from the community when it succeeds. By forcing top-down objectives upon a community, you cripple its development. If early on you start demanding your community buys more of your product, gives you feedback, promotes what you sell, you hurt the development of the community. It doesn't matter how subtly or *honestly* you try to do it.

DEVELOPING A COMMUNITY STRATEGY

A strategy is comprised of the following five steps:

1. **Data collection.** The first step is to collect data about the audience and the current progress and health of the community. This includes both quantitative and qualitative data. Collecting this data is a time-consuming but important task. It's the single, most reliable way to make sure you're doing the right thing. Anything else is guessing.

2. **Analyze data.** Once you've collected data, you need to analyze how the community is progressing through the prisms of growth, activity, and sense of community. You need to identify the health of the community and its ROI. This doesn't take long.

3. **Establish the goals.** Based upon where the community is now, you can use theory to determine where the community needs to go next. You set goals for each of the other elements within the community management

framework and targets they can be measured against.

4. **Create an action plan.** Now you have the goals, you need to develop an action plan to get there. This should be broken down into a very specific three-month calendar (week by week), and a broad 12-month plan (month by month). Highlight what needs to be done at the beginning of each week by creating a day-by-day plan.

5. **Track progress and ensure accountability.** Finally, you need to track progress towards these goals and ensure none of the goals are missed. You might also identify any obstacles that prevent these goals from being realized.

Can you spot the trend here? You're not making up a strategy. Anyone can make up a strategy that sounds terrific but is either unrealistic, is not supported by data or theory, or is difficult to execute. It's far more difficult and more reliable, to create a strategy based upon data and theory.

So let's review the theory behind how communities develop. This forms the basis for any strategy.

THE COMMUNITY LIFECYCLE

Online communities (and offline communities too) develop along a relatively fixed path. They start small and steadily grow larger. They have different needs at different stages. The community lifecycle explains this development; it also acts as a map.

This map tells you where your community is now and where it needs to go next. The lifecycle directly dictates your actions. You respond to the unique needs of the community at each stage.

The biggest mistake made by organizations is ignoring this fixed path. Too many organizations try to jump ahead several stages along the lifecycle without realizing the negative consequences of doing so. For example, they see a mature community such as Patient's Like Me (healthcare) or Mumsnet (parenting) and decide they need to be really big to succeed. What they ignore is the path they took to be successful. They confuse the end result with the process. The process is to start small and grow gradually. In the early stages you need to focus on very specific things.

If organizations don't acknowledge the community lifecycle, they have no way of establishing realistic expectations for their community strategy. Many online communities are killed before they have had the opportunity to be a success. If you try to take a shortcut, you will focus on the wrong metrics and not properly develop the community for the long-term.

What is the community lifecycle?

Iriberri and Leroy (2009) did not invent the community lifecycle, but they were the first to review thousands of academic articles on community development and lay out a clear set of stages and success factors.

A variety of practitioners (including my company) have refined the process to further develop communities. The lifecycle forms the basis for community development and shows what you should be working towards at any particular time.

THERE ARE FOUR STAGES TO THE COMMUNITY LIFECYCLE:

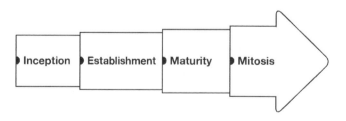

Each stage is separated from the next by growth, activity, and the sense of community.

	INCEPTION	ESTABLISHMENT	MATURITY	MITOSIS
Growth	50 - 100% direct growth via the community manager	50 – 90% referral growth	90%+ referral growth	Variable
Activity	0 – 50% of activity initiated by members	50 – 90% of activity initiated by the community	90 – 99% of activity initiated by community members	Activity dips to between 50 – 99% of activity initiated by the community
Sense of Community	N/A	0 – 24	24 - 72	72 - 96

STAGE 1: INCEPTION

The inception stage starts when you begin interacting with the target audience and ends with the community achieving a critical mass of growth and activity.

Critical mass

Critical mass is a term from nuclear physics defined as the minimum amount of fissile material to sustain a nuclear chain reaction. This term has become co-opted by social scientists as a *tipping point* used to describe the moment any social activity becomes self-sustaining.

For your purposes, critical mass is when the level of growth and activity in the community *continues to increase* without your direct involvement. This point is numerically defined as when more than 50% of growth and activity is generated by the community (as opposed to the community manager).

The sole goal of the inception stage is to achieve critical mass by cultivating a small group of highly active members in the community. This group becomes the foundation upon which to build the community. Unless a small, active, group is established it is impossible to develop a successful long-term community.

The tasks you perform in the inception stage of the community lifecycle will be significantly different from those you undertake in the maturity phase. You shouldn't be doing the same job from one year to the next. Your role evolves with the community. During this phase, you should focus upon micro-level activities designed to solicit a high level of engagement from a relatively small number of individuals. It is important to establish momentum, a sense of possibility, and a regular amount of activity from members at this stage of the lifecycle (Wenger, 2003; Iriberri and Leroy, 2009).

During inception, you need to focus on performing a relatively small number of tasks many times. These include:

Direct Growth

You should be individually inviting people you have developed relationships with to join and participate in the community. These relationships should have been developed in the conceptualization stage. Those members you interview to learn more about how to create a community should then become the first members of the community.

These invitations will usually take place by e-mail, although personal invitations at events and other channels are also acceptable. Directly inviting people you know is the most reliable source of early growth in online communities.

Stimulated Activity

You will also be stimulating activity in the community with a three-fold approach. First, you will be initiating discussions on topics that research has shown members are interested in.

Discussions can be scheduled in advance; mix those that are designed to convey information with those that affect members on a psychological level, such as bonding/status-jockeying discussions.

In addition, you should be prompting members to participate in these discussions. This requires individually reaching out to members through the site or by e-mail and letting them know that their opinion on the discussion would be valued.

Your goal is to get these members into the habit of regularly visiting the community to see the responses to their own posts. It takes time until visiting a community becomes a habit. Until then, members need frequent reminders to participate. Automated reminders are not enough.

LITTLE HOLLYWOOD GIRL	rosiebarm	2	11 days
HERNANDO'S HIDE-AWAY by Don & Phil	J200bert	3	11 days
Poems,prayers and promises	J200bert	6	11 days
Till I kissed you	everly	15	11 days
ILLINOIS BY EVERLY BROTHERS	rosiebarm	4	11 days
Nothing Matters But You	rosiebarm	3	11 days
Phil "Don't Cha Know"	bledune	4	11 days
The Blues Don and Phil	rosiebarm	10	11 days
WHEN SNOWFLAKES FALL IN SUMMER	rosiebarm	20	13 days
TO SHOW I LOVE YOU	rosiebarm	1	13 days
The Brothers at Work	rosiebarm	5	13 days
ALWAYS ITS YOU- EVERLY BROTHERS	rosiebarm	3	13 days
PHIL EVERLY WITH DION	rosiebarm	4	14 days

During the early stage of managing online communities, the community founder initiates most of the activity.

At this stage you should also invest time in building good relationships with members. Reach out to individual members and identify ways to be of assistance or continue to learn what members are most interested in. This ensures a steady flow of activity, feedback on current activities, and opportunities to initiate activities in the future.

Signs of development

As the community begins to develop, members will invite others in their online and offline social networks to join the community. A gradually increasing number of new members will arrive without you inviting them.

In addition, members will begin initiating their own discussions in the community. This number should steadily increase. Members will also begin replying to discussions without you directly prompting them. Visiting the community starts to become a habit.

At this stage, you should continue to undertake the same activities as before (and at the same level as before). A common mistake is to begin shifting activities to more micro-level activities too soon. Until critical mass has been reached and sustained, you should have a precise focus upon the four tasks I have just highlighted:

1. Invite members to join the community.
2. Initiate discussions members will be interested in.
3. Prompt members to participate in discussions.
4. Build relationships with members.

This phase can last anywhere from one to nine months. Any longer typically indicates a development problem. It shows the community is not naturally taking off and there is either a conceptual problem or a tactical problem.

If community members do not invite others to join, or initiate activity without you directly prompting them, this is a sign that either the community concept is wrong (the community isn't about a topic members are interested in), or you're using the wrong tactics. This may be due to errors in your approach or not testing different approaches.

In the latter example, the way you interact with members, invite people to join, or initiate discussions is wrong. Approaches that are too long, for example, or discussions that are not relevant enough to members, are unlikely to generate a lot of activity. In addition, in some sectors approaches that are too formal or feel pushy also fail to solicit the desired activity.

STAGE 2: ESTABLISHMENT

The establishment phase of the online community lifecycle begins when the community has reached critical mass: the community itself generates more than 50% of growth and activity. The establishment phase ends when members are generating over 90% of growth and activity in the community.

Once the establishment phase has been reached, your role gradually shifts from the micro-level tasks that focus on individual members at a time to more macro-level activities (tasks that affect several members at a time). These activities include those that sustain growth, activity, and develop a sense of community.

Referral and promotional growth

You should now gradually shift away from direct growth and encourage referral and promotional growth (members inviting their friends and coverage in media outlets read by the target audience).

Referral growth tactics will include ownership/involvement level ideas that encourage members to invite their friends. For example, you establish an event/goal that members participate in, increase a sense of ownership and thus invite other people in their social network to join the community. Or you might focus upon sharing content/discussions within the community. You will also spend more time converting newcomers into regular members of the community.

You will also have some promotional activities during this time. This might be outreach to bloggers/magazines, issuing statements on behalf of the community, hosting events that involve interests of your target audience.

Don't leave growth to chance; you have to proactively stimulate it.

Scaling activity

Most organizations allow their communities to grow until they become unmanageable. Don't let this happen to you. Embed scaling processes early in the development lifecycle. Prepare now to have a big community later. This involves recruiting volunteers, developing the platform, and optimizing areas of the site.

The community manager will also have to spend more time on moderation: resolving disputes between members, concentrating and dissipating activity, removing spam/inappropriate material, highlighting the most popular discussions/activities.

Sense of community

At this stage of the lifecycle, the community manager must begin to introduce elements that increase the sense of community felt among members. This usually involves initiating events and activities as shared experiences, introducing a community constitution, promoting the community in other media, and documenting the community history.

The community manager needs members to feel they are part of a community together to sustain a high level of activity among members. It keeps people returning to the community to see what's new, as opposed to only visiting when notified of a reaction to their own post.

In addition, content will play an important role in further developing the community. Content can help develop a community narrative, highlight the top members in the community, create a social order within the community, and (akin to a local newspaper) increase the sense of *togetherness* felt by members.

Signs of development

During this phase of the lifecycle, you should see growing levels of growth and activity, which should be closely correlated. Growth should increasingly come from referrals/word-of-mouth activity.

In addition, the community should continue to generate an increasing amount of its own activity. The level of responses per discussion should continue to rise, and the number of discussions initiated by members should also steadily increase.

						Most read	Most commented

Topic	Discussions	Posts	Last post
General discussions			
Introductions			
New to the community? Introduce yourself here.	310	1385	Microvascular angina - coronary ... by shirley burrell 1 hour 11 min ago
The Social (off topic chat)			
A place to chat and relax.	32	234	Have you stopped snoring? by Tracy Mason 10 hours 34 min ago
Feedback on the BHF			
Do you think we could do something better? Let us know	10	85	Community feedback by ourmike 29/07/2012 - 4:14am

- Shape the future of the NHS 593 reads
- Embarking on your next running challenge.. Why not share your training tips with other members of the team! 486 reads
- Help dealing with hubby. x 335 reads
- Hello All 335 reads
- Mum recently had heart attack. Drugs make her feel sick and have headaches 300 reads

A community in the establishment phase should show continued growth and development, in addition to a sense of community. This is often reflected in a growing amount of off-topic/social chatter.

Signs that a sense of community is developing among members may include in-jokes, a continuation of discussions beyond the immediate subject matter, an increasing amount of direct contact between members, higher levels of self-disclosure in debates and other signals of familiarity between members.

Broad lists of tasks

During this phase of the online community lifecycle, the number of tasks you focus upon will broaden and you need to shift your time accordingly. These tasks include:

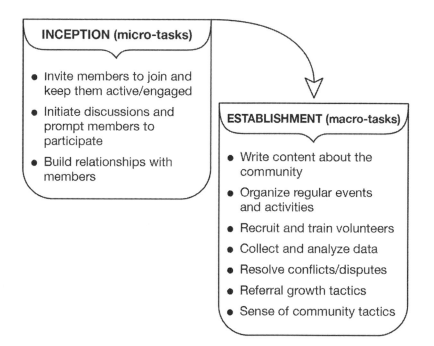

The objective of this phase is to continue increasing growth and activity, develop a limited sense of community, and provide the basis for sustainable development of the community.

This final point is important. It would be difficult, for example, for anyone to handle a community membership numbering over 100,000 active members without support. The processes that allow a community to scale must begin relatively early in the community's lifecycle.

Potential problems

A drop in growth or activity indicates a potential problem for the community. If growth increases but the activity drops, then members are becoming less active than before or a smaller number of members are accounting for an increasingly larger share of activity.

Tracking relevant data is important to spot these potential issues. If you identify an issue, you can initiate activities designed to change this trend before you lose too many members. Once you enter a dip, it's hard to avoid a death spiral (less activity begets less activity).

It is also common for community managers to switch roles too early: to go from micro- to macro-level activities too rapidly as opposed to gradually shifting roles as the measurement of growth and activity shows progress.

STAGE 3: MATURITY

The maturity phase of the online community lifecycle begins when members of the community are generating 90% or more of activity/growth, and there is a limited sense of community.

This is measured through growth, activity, and sense of community metrics. The maturity phase ends when the community has a highly developed sense of community, but the level of activity or sense of community among members has plateaued.

Most familiar online communities are in their maturity phase. They are established, highly active, and have a highly developed sense of community. They also merit a lot of attention within their ecosystem.

This final element, external attention, is common among mature communities. They become the definitive place for those interested in that topic. Mumsnet is the definitive community for parents in the UK. Techcrunch is the definitive community for start-up companies. 4Chan has a thriving online community for online hackers/pranksters.

By this stage, you should only rarely be initiating discussions, prompting people to participate, or engaging in any micro-tasks besides those that facilitate relationships with members/volunteers. You should only do this to *fill in the gaps* (i.e. when there is a lull in activity, it makes sense for you to prompt a few discussions).

Now you should be focused solely upon macro-level activities that have the biggest long-term impact upon the majority of members in the community. This includes scaling processes, events/activities, content, optimizing of the platform, developing a strong sense of community, and increasing the profile of the community outside of the platform.

Your volunteers or additional staff should now be handling the micro-activities undertaken in the previous stages of the lifecycle (e.g. conflict resolution, removing spam, responding to member queries). You need to focus on the bigger things.

During this phase, there will usually be a plateau in growth. This is the natural consequence of the community reaching its maximum potential. There are only so many people who can be interested in the community's topic. Once this figure has been reached, further growth is not possible.

In addition, there will eventually be a plateau in activity— when members are as active as they can possibly be. This is the outcome of members who have a strong sense of community and dedicate as much time to the topic as they possibly can. The goal at this stage is to sustain this high level of activity and increase the sense of community among members.

A plateau is not a major cause for concern. It is the natural and final evolution of a successful online community. You should only be concerned when there is a decline, especially a sustained decline. I cover this topic in the mitosis phase of the community lifecycle.

Growth

During this phase, all growth will come from referrals/word-of-mouth activity (such as sharing content/discussions, networking at events, or generally being a well-known community within the sector), and the organization's promotional efforts.

The community manager helps gain publicity in major outlets and develops a system by which all members feel a sense of ownership over areas of the community.

This will involve ensuring the community is frequently mentioned within its sector and also making the community influential within its realm. For example, by releasing regular statements related to relevant issues and working with influencers to implement desirable change within the sector. Mumsnet frequently campaigns on behalf of its members.

Mumsnet proactively runs campaigns on issues its members care deeply about. The success rate is remarkably high.

Activity

The level of activity per member will peak during the maturity phase of the community lifecycle. The community will become highly responsive, and you should focus on reviewing what areas of the site are used and optimizing the most used features.

In the maturity phase of the lifecycle, the level of activity is extremely high and the community is well known in its sector.

You also need to closely analyze the process through which a newcomer becomes a regular and take steps to enhance that process based on data, not a haphazard series of actions.

Sense of community

The activities you undertake at this stage blur the lines between growth, activity, and sense of community. Releasing statements on behalf of the community, for example, achieves all three: it promotes the community, it increases activity from members talking about the issue, and makes members feel a greater sense of community from the influence their community has upon its ecosystem.

A list of activities at this stage is below:

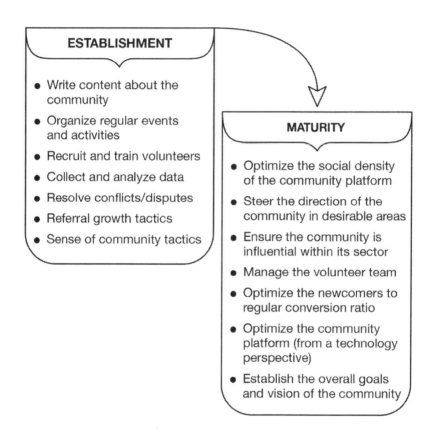

ESTABLISHMENT

- Write content about the community
- Organize regular events and activities
- Recruit and train volunteers
- Collect and analyze data
- Resolve conflicts/disputes
- Referral growth tactics
- Sense of community tactics

MATURITY

- Optimize the social density of the community platform
- Steer the direction of the community in desirable areas
- Ensure the community is influential within its sector
- Manage the volunteer team
- Optimize the newcomers to regular conversion ratio
- Optimize the community platform (from a technology perspective)
- Establish the overall goals and vision of the community

The objective at this stage is, counter-intuitively, to hit the plateau, the point where the community has reached its initial maximum potential. Everyone in the sector should know of you, your members are highly active, and there is a deep sense of community among members.

STAGE 4: MITOSIS

The mitosis phase of the online community lifecycle begins when the community is almost entirely self-sustaining and ends when it begins to break up into smaller, more focused, online communities.

Not all communities progress to this phase. For example, my friend Susan runs Park Slope Parents, a community for a few thousand parents in Brooklyn, New York. Her community is highly active, but will never grow so big it needs to split into multiple sub-groups. It has a much smaller potential audience than a larger community like Mumsnet.

Mumsnet targets parents throughout the UK; Park Slope Parents is just for a relatively small area in New York. Mumsnet has a potential audience in the millions; Park Slope Parents has a potential audience of a few thousand.

Susan has seen this community through to the maturity phase of the lifecycle. She's maximized the potential of that community. Therefore, it won't enter the mitosis stage of the lifecycle.

NOTE: As of October 1, 2011, membership requires a $35 fee.
This fee gives you discounts to over 340 (and growing) local businesses and
services CHECK THE DISCOUNTS HERE

Message History

	Jan	Feb	Mar	Apr	May	Jun	Jul	Aug	Sep	Oct	Nov	Dec
2012	1676	1367	1677	1332	1390	1397	1237	35				
2011	1900	1710	2023	1605	1591	1769	1263	1503	1649	1590	1472	1269
2010	1554	1428	1635	1428	1527	1404	1328	1188	1268	1457	1424	1594
2009	1851	1430	1638	1869	1480	1189	965	868	1025	1129	1400	1500
2008	1712	1719	1710	1604	1778	1766	1550	1337	1586	1520	1453	1395
2007	1747	1618	2084	1539	1952	1764	1482	1271	1633	1754	1650	1249
2006	1413	1047	1511	1145	1166	1354	1109	1426	1564	1490	1367	1293
2005	938	847	1333	1477	1165	1069	924	1063	1162	1152	1273	1213
2004	966	841	1140	1130	1351	1321	1505	1609	1017	978	793	894
2003	273	197	446	526	602	577	629	556	800	893	829	863
2002							22	48	178	339	176	172

Join This Group!

*Not all communities advance to mitosis. The message history for Park Slope
Parents shows a plateau since 2007 without any significant decline.*

If you have a large potential audience (or a large existing
community), once the plateau has been reached, you need to
shift your role again from optimizing to facilitating multiple,
smaller, online communities. The objective of this phase is
to sustain and increase the level of both activity, and sense
of community.

Growth
During this phase of the lifecycle, the growth to the community as a whole should remain consistent, but the growth to
the smaller sub-groups should be growing as in the inception
stage. This means, initially, the co-founders of the sub-group

will invite new members, usually through existing contacts made in the community.

You may also have to stimulate growth by mentioning new groups through content/discussions, and by hosting events and activities for these groups. Each of these sub-groups should endeavor to achieve a critical mass within the first three months of existence. You will need to train people to manage these groups and provide support when necessary.

Activity

The overall level of activity to the community should increase as members reform around stronger common interests (social circles, niche interests within the topic). Each group should be smaller, but more members will have the opportunity to be involved.

There may be a brief, short-term dip in activity as members gradually move from the broad topic into a niche group based around their activities.

You need to focus on identifying the potential sub-groups at this stage. Identify the topics or interests that have continually arisen within the community, and then create a group specifically for these individuals. This group might be a forum category or any other place within the community platform where people can interact.

In ScienceForums, members each have several sub-groups they participate in. The broad topic 'science' has been artfully broken into highly active sub-groups.

Alternatively, you may identify social groups that have developed within the community and build areas within the platform just for close groups of friends. These groups might be elders, newcomers, those who have attended particular events (events especially are a good place for members to bond).

You might want to look at your original audience overview to identify clusters of people who share the same demographic, habitual, or psychographic traits. These are ideal categories for developing sub-groups.

Sense of community

The sense of community at this stage will dip before rising considerably. Past a certain stage, it's impossible for all members to feel a sense of connection with everyone. Breaking the community into smaller sub-groups helps sustain these connections. Fewer people are more active in the community.

You should spend considerable time helping boost the sense of community in each of these groups. It is therefore important not to launch multiple groups at a single time, but to gradually increase the number of groups in the community.

Mitosis phase tasks

During this phase of the community lifecycle, the community manager balances the role of sustaining a healthy community in the maturity phase with developing self-sustaining groups.

Note in the tasks below, as in the previous phases, there is a gradual shift from the maturity level tasks to the mitosis level tasks. This should not be an abrupt change. It may be possible not to split the entire community into sub-groups, just elements/people within the community.

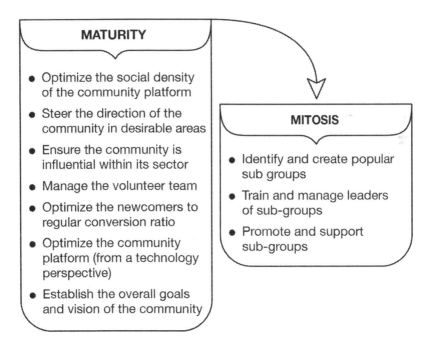

MATURITY

- Optimize the social density of the community platform
- Steer the direction of the community in desirable areas
- Ensure the community is influential within its sector
- Manage the volunteer team
- Optimize the newcomers to regular conversion ratio
- Optimize the community platform (from a technology perspective)
- Establish the overall goals and vision of the community

MITOSIS

- Identify and create popular sub groups
- Train and manage leaders of sub-groups
- Promote and support sub-groups

While the number of mitosis tasks looks light, it is a highly repetitive process. For instance, the amount of managing of sub-group leaders will steadily increase throughout the lifespan of the community (perhaps until you're managing the people who manage the sub-group leaders).

Signs of development

As the community advances into the mitosis phase of the community lifecycle, an increasing number of successful niche groups/topics should be visible within the community. These should be independently run with only small assistance from you.

Over time, these sub-groups should be organizing regular events, maintaining a regular content schedule, and become relatively self-sustaining, close-knit, entities within the community.

Potential dangers

As I mentioned earlier, it is common for community managers to let their community become too big and too active without proper structure. Past a certain number of active members in a community, it becomes impossible for a high level of familiarity to persist. Members will know fewer and fewer other participants. Therefore, the overall sense of community in the community begins to decrease. This often leads to less ownership over the community and eventually a lower number of participating members.

Similarly, once a community becomes too active, it becomes difficult for members to stay abreast of what's new and popular in the community. It becomes difficult to follow the overall narrative of the community. This is often referred to as 'information overload' (Jones et al., 2004).

A member used to catching up on 10 missed messages feels less motivation to catch up on 50 or 500 messages. It becomes harder to find the messages that will be most relevant.

If you fail to use your data to recognize these situations, it can result in the number of members gradually declining to a small group who retain a limited sense of community with one another.

Another potential danger at this stage is top-down community planning. Instead of reacting to interests that have risen naturally within the community, those that have clearly gained a high level of participation, the community attempts a top-down approach to try and facilitate multiple groups at once. This approach is not suited to community development.

FireArmsTalk

Creating multiple groups rapidly dissipates activity within the community. This can cause a sharp, uncontrolled, drop in the level of activity. It can fail to develop any group to critical mass. Sub-groups need to be nurtured to advance past the inception stage. It's important to develop these individually before making a huge change at this stage.

ESTABLISHING STRATEGY

Your strategy depends upon where your community is in its lifecycle. In the following section, I outline the precise formula to identify where your community is in the lifecycle.

Growth

To determine whether growth has reached critical mass, you need the following data:

1. Number of members the community manager invited to join.
2. Number of members that joined as a result of these invitations.
3. Number of members that joined as a result of other promotional activity by the community manager.
4. Total number of new registered members during this time.

When members join a community, you want to identify where they joined from, either through a question in the registration form or by tracking the individual user journeys on Google Analytics and calculating it as a percentage of total.

Critical mass of growth is achieved when the total number of newly registered members in the community is *double* the number of members that have joined through your direct invitations (both one-to-one and to your existing mailing lists/audiences).

SPECIFICALLY, YOU WANT TO KNOW:

Total number of registered members within 30 days
- *Less* members directly invited
- *Less* members joined through activities stimulated by the community manager

You can plot this in a table and graph as shown below:

Progression Metrics	Jan	Feb	Mar	Apr	May	Jun	Jul	Aug	Sept	Oct	Nov	Dec	Jan
- Total number of new members	24	61	62	79	112	72	117	213	381	240	227	247	271
- New members invited by CMGR	21	27	33	28	33	27	21	27	38	11	11	8	21
- New members from organic channels	3	34	29	51	79	45	96	186	243	229	216	239	250
% of members by the community	12.50%	55.74%	46.77%	64.56%	70.54%	62.50%	82.05%	87.32%	86.48%	95.42%	95.15%	96.76%	92.25%

Growth Figures

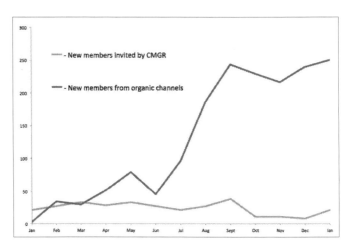

New Members Graph

In the graph above, notice that the community didn't achieve critical mass until early March.

Activity

To determine activity for the context of the community life-cycle, you follow a similar approach. Review the total amount of activity within the community and subtract this by the level of activity the community manager stimulated.

For example, if the outcome surpasses the amount of activity initiated by the community manager, you have achieved a critical mass.

In larger online communities, it may be difficult to individually calculate this. Therefore, you may need to use a sample of 20 discussions you initiated, 20 discussions selected using a systematic technique, dividing the outcome by 100 and then multiplying this by the total number of discussions for each. The more discussions you sample from here, the more accurate you will be.

YOU CALCULATE:

Total number of posts
- *Less* posts from the community manager
- *Less* responses to discussions initiated by the community manager

Plot this in a table and graph as shown below:

Activity KPIs	Jan	Feb	Mar	Apr	May	Jun	Jul	Aug	Sept	Oct	Nov	Dec
Total number of posts per month	57	78	91	57	88	114	184	183	175	262	392	720
Total number of new discussions	26	31	31	39	46	53	48	66	54	98	140	162
Discussions initiated by CMGR	22	27	23	27	22	25	26	25	25	25	21	22
# responses to discussions initiated by CMGR	47	61	67	54	57	33	77	57	55	61	80	81

Activity KPI figures

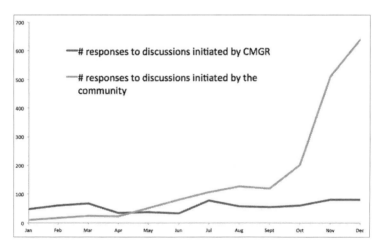

In the above graph, you can see the community reached critical mass of activity after about 4.5 months.

Sense of community

Sense of community is a concept with great history. It was first properly articulated in McMillan and Chavis's 1986 paper *Psychological Sense of Community*. McMillan and Chavis summarized a range of literature to produce four key factors inherent in developing a strong sense of community:

1. **Membership.** Do members feel a sense of identification with one another?

2. **Influence.** Do members feel influenced by the community and influential within the community?

3. **Integration and fulfillment of needs.** Are members' needs being met? Are those needs aligned with the needs of the community?

4. **Shared emotional connection.** Do members share an emotional connection with one another?

It's important to track your members' sense of community. A community can have a good level of growth and high levels of engagement but fail to develop relationships between members. This is the case for many customer-service-based communities.

The sense of community measures the relationships that have developed between members and whether members *feel* they are part of a community. It's that *feeling* that leads to increased loyalty, greater likelihood to purchase from your company, increased potential to recommend to others, give you feedback, and so forth.

Ultimately, more than any other metric, it is the sense of community that will drive the positive ROI for your organization.

How to measure sense of community

Chavis and others later produced a sense of community index, to measure the sense of a community. It is a survey, which means members need to be invited to participate.

The index asks people to rate whether they agree with the following statements on a scale of 0 for "not at all" to 3 for "completely":

1. *I get important needs of mine met because I am part of this community.*
2. *Community members and I value the same things.*
3. *This community has been successful in getting the needs of its members met.*
4. *Being a member of this community makes me feel good.*
5. *When I have a problem, I can talk about it with members of this community.*
6. *People in this community have similar needs, priorities, and goals.*
7. *I can trust people in this community.*
8. *I can recognize most of the members of this community.*
9. *Most community members know me.*
10. *This community has symbols and expressions of membership such as clothes, signs, art, architecture, logos, landmarks, and flags that people can recognize.*
11. *I put a lot of time and effort into being part of this community.*
12. *Being a member of this community is a part of my identity.*
13. *Fitting into this community is important to me.*
14. *This community can influence other communities.*
15. *I care about what other community members think of me.*
16. *I have influence over what this community is like.*
17. *If there is a problem in this community, members can get it solved.*
18. *This community has good leaders.*
19. *It is very important to me to be a part of this community.*

20. I am with other community members a lot and enjoy being with them.

21. I expect to be a part of this community for a long time.

22. Members of this community have shared important events together, such as holidays, celebrations, or disasters.

23. I feel hopeful about the future of this community.

24. Members of this community care about each other.

THE ANSWERS CORRESPOND TO THE FOLLOWING ASPECTS OF SENSE OF COMMUNITY:

- Subscales Reinforcement of Needs = Q1 + Q2 + Q3 + Q4 + Q5 + Q6
- Membership = Q7 + Q8 + Q9 + Q10 + Q11 + Q12
- Influence = Q13 + Q14 + Q15 + Q16 + Q17 + Q18
- Shared Emotional Connection = Q19 + Q20 + Q21 + Q22 + Q23 + Q24

The trouble with surveys

A problem with using surveys is the limit to how frequently they can be used. Asking members to undertake the same survey every month will cause fatigue and possibly irritate members.

Therefore, either measure a small sample of the total members each month and rotate those approached, or measure the sense of community at less frequent intervals, for example six to 12 months.

Survey collection techniques

While the later approach might be easiest, problems in the community might not emerge for some time. In addition, even these time frames can irritate members. It is best to develop several unique segments of members stratified upon their date of registration. Rotate the survey so members receive the same survey no more than once a year.

It is important to do the survey correctly. The results would be significantly biased if the survey was posted on the site and members were invited to participate. Those members who are most active and feel the strongest sense of community are most likely to participate. The members who feel the lowest sense of community are least likely to participate.

So you need a stratified sample that splits the members by the date joined and then samples those members. For example, if 5% of active members have been in the community for five years, 9% for four years, 17% for three years, 15% for two years, 21% for one year and 33% have joined within the past year, then the number of survey responses should reflect the same percentages.

This means the community must list members by the date they joined, find those which are still active, and then send this quantity of members the survey. Based upon the quantity responses, it may be necessary to send out more surveys to meet the quota for each category.

Be sure to use a stratified sample of the different clusters of members in the community (use either the level of activity or the date members joined).

Like growth and activity, collect this data and plot it on a graph as shown below:

Sense of community	Spring 10	Summer 10	Autumn 10	Winter 10	Spring 11	Summer 11	Autumn 11
# Members responded to survey	27	42	45	44	78	77	41
- total reinformcement of needs	81	126	180	176	468	539	328
- avg. reinforcement of needs	3	3	4	4	6	7	8
- total membership	108	84	225	176	312	462	246
- avg. membership	4	2	5	4	4	6	6
- total influence	54	84	135	308	780	924	451
- avg. influence	2	2	3	7	10	12	11
- total shared emotional connection	27	42	90	88	78	308	123
- avg. shared emotional connection	1	1	2	2	1	4	3
Total score	270	336	630	748	1638	2233	1148
Average result	10	8	14	17	21	29	28
% of total	10%	8%	15%	18%	22%	30%	29%

Sense of Community KPIs

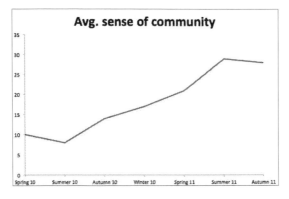

Average sense of community

Turning strategy into action

Now you have the theoretical understanding of community development, you can develop an action plan to further develop the community. The action plan is a clear document that highlights what needs to be achieved and when it needs to be achieved (and in large-scale terms, who needs to achieve it).

This plans ensures focus and accountability. It keeps the community manager focused upon the important task of *developing* the community as opposed to *maintaining* the community. Even the best community managers often struggle to resist the lure of reactive work (responding to isolated occurrences) as opposed to advancing the community as a whole.

Using the community management framework you can place all community management activities in to one of eight categories (see chart on page 17). Within each category are specific tasks for the community manager. The action plan shifts the balance towards the tasks that are most important at each particular time.

As a practical example, if you have a community with reasonable levels of growth and activity, but a low sense of community, the strategy would emphasize the elements that constitute the sense of community (membership, influence, integration of needs, and shared emotional connection).

Time allocation guide

Over the years, I have compiled a rough estimate of how much time a community manager should spend on each activity. To develop the action plan, multiply the total number of hours available by the percentage, based upon which stage of the lifecycle your community is presently in.

	INCEPTION	ESTABLISHMENT	MATURITY	MITOSIS
Strategy	5%	5%	5%	5%
Growth	45%	25%	10%	25%
Moderation	30%	20%	25%	20%
Content	0%	10%	10%	10%
Relationships	15%	15%	15%	15%
Events and Activities	0%	10%	10%	10%
Business Integration	0%	5%	10%	10%
Technology	5%	10%	15%	5%

For example, a community manager with 40 working hours to spend on the community in the establishment phase would spend two hours a week on strategy (data collection/analysis), 10 hours on growth, eight hours on moderation, four hours each on content, events/activities, and the user experience, six hours on relationship development and two hours on business integration.

The proactive first principle

To ensure the focus remains on developing the community, apply the *proactive-first* principle: unless there is an urgent technical issue in the community (or a life-threatening situation), the community manager will undertake the *proactive* tasks first.

An average day

An average day for a community in the establishment phase might be:

- **9am – 10am:** Creating content
- **10am – 12pm:** Growth activities
- **1pm – 2pm:** Organizing events
- **2pm – 3.30pm:** Moderation
- **3:30pm – 5:00pm:** Relationship development

Naturally, this is a utopian version of a community manager's day. In real life, an array of issues will most likely arise that disrupts this schedule significantly. However, the focus on what needs to be accomplished and the approximate balance of time needed to complete each activity is essential to effective community management.

Some tasks here are better batched together as opposed to spread throughout the week. For example, it might make sense to create most content in the beginning of the week, or allocate two hours on Friday to collecting data, as opposed to 20 minutes every day.

User experience activities, business integration, strategy, and most content are better batched into blocks of several hours on specific days. The remaining tasks are better spread throughout the remaining days.

Then you need to drop the specific activities into these blocks of time. This list isn't comprehensive, but does identify what should be achieved on any particular day.

STRATEGY	GROWTH	MODERATION	CONTENT
Collecting Data	Direct invitations	Guidelines	Creating calendar
Analyzing data	Promotion	Social density	Informative content
Establishing goals	Referrals/WOM	Initiating discussions	Entertaining content
Communicating goals	Search/ Miscellaneous	Resolving disputes	Persuasive/ inspiring content
Ecosystem scanning	Converting newcomers into regulars	Steering the community	User generated content
		Soliciting responses	

RELATIONSHIPS	EVENTS/ ACTIVITIES	BUSINESS INTEGRATION	USER EXPERIENCE
Personal participation	Online and regular	Engaging employees	Maintenance
Cultivating volunteers	Online and irregular	Tremendous value exchanges	Future scanning
Befriending key members	Offline and regular	Price	Optimization
	Offline and irregular	Products	Miscellaneous
	Content and discussions	Promotion	
		Place	
		People	
		Process	

Within each of these lists, you can pick out the tasks most appropriate to your community. The average day becomes a more specific day:

- **9am – 10am:** Content: Write entertaining content about recent community activity and informative content about upcoming events in the sector. Update the community history page.

- **10am – 12pm:** Growth activities: Directly invite 10 people with a shared interest in (x) to join. Reach out to previous invitees and check how they're integrating with the community.

- **1pm – 2pm:** Event organizing: Plan upcoming regular event series on improvement in the topic. Find four guest speakers and schedule/announce the event.

- **2pm – 3.30pm:** Moderation: Initiate self-disclosure discussions to increase familiarity about how members first became interested in the topic. Highlight the new most popular topics. Solicit responses to yesterday's discussions from newly arrived members.

- **3:30pm – 5:00pm:** Relationship development. Reach out to three members who have made a unique contribution and see if they would like to write a regular article on that topic.

This is merely an example. By undertaking the process, however, you can maintain a forward-looking approach to community development. The goal is to keep focusing on *developing* the community, not maintaining it.

Community health metrics

Unfortunately, life gets a little more complicated. Just tracking progress won't reveal some major problems. You also need to track the overall health of the community, the level of responsiveness, interaction, and liveliness.

In the following chapters, I explore each element of the framework in greater depth and highlight how you can combine data and theory to optimize every single task.

CHAPTER 2

Growth

You are responsible for growing the community. Too many community managers wait for members to arrive via search traffic or other serendipitous coincidence rather than pro-actively growing their community.

But what sort of growth do you want? Do you need to re-plenish members you're losing? Expand the community? Or penetrate further into the audience you already have?

Remember, growth doesn't mean merely persuading someone to visit the site. It includes converting a newcomer to a regular member of the community. You must welcome newcomers, ensure they make that first contribution to the community, and keep them participating.

ANALYZING YOUR CURRENT LEVELS OF GROWTH

You need to know whether the community is growing or shrink-ing. You also want to know the speed of growth. In *Bowling Alone* (2000), Robert Putnam explained the main reason for the rapid decline in a number of once-thriving community-based orga-nizations is a lack of new blood replacing existing members. This problem is even more epidemic in online communities.

In Putnam's review of communities, membership was local and relatively static. Members usually left when they moved away, which was rare, or when they died (or became too frail to participate), which was also rare.

In online communities, membership is far more dynamic. Members leave when they get bored with the topic, find new jobs, have new life commitments, or simply when something new comes along. A considerable emphasis needs to be placed upon both 1) retaining existing members and 2) ensuring a steady supply of fresh blood to replace departing members.

You need to calculate whether the number of active members in the community is growing or shrinking. You also need to determine the best sources of growth to optimize your promotional activities and how newcomers progress into regulars.

Note that I am referring to *active* members in a community, people who have made a post within the previous 30 days. The number of *registered* members is a meaningless statistic; it doesn't reveal how many members are active. It's easy to get a lot of people to register; it's harder to keep them active after six months. The other problem with registered members is that members don't delete their accounts when they leave a community. Therefore, the number of registered members continues to rise regardless of what the community manager does.

That's great news if you're tracking how many members actually become active in your community. It's bad news if you're trying to meaningfully develop your community. Imagine if your community ever hits its 50th birthday (Surprised? Don't be! The WELL, one of the internet's oldest communities, recently celebrated its 30th birthday)—a number of your members will have since died. Yet, you would continue to count them as members of the community.

Now replace '*died*' with lost interest in the topic, got a new job, had new life priorities, moved away, etc. You will forever continue to count all these people as members. You might laugh, but the oldest internet communities are hitting their 30th birthday.

So don't count the people who performed the mere act of completing a registration form as members. Only count those who made an active contribution to the community within the past month.

This number is useful because it reflects your actions. It's a number that can go up and down. Scary, perhaps, but useful.

USING DATA TO OPTIMIZE GROWTH

The best way to grow a community is to target segments (or clusters) that share a demographic, habitual, or psychographic attribute.

I suggest launching your community with a focus on just one of these segments. Once you've reached critical mass, you can begin expanding by identifying and approaching new segments to join. You can cater the community activities specifically to this audience.

For example, let's say you run a community for comic book fans. After an analysis of your target audience, you identify several different segments. There is a rather large cluster that lives in Boston, another cluster that lives in London, and another in Idaho. You also notice that there are people who prefer niche anime comics, others who like adult comics, and still another group that is deeply interested in historical comics like Superman, Spiderman, or even *Radioactive man!*

You notice that there isn't already an established community for comic book fans in Boston, so you expand your community in this direction. You identify several people in Boston and conduct psychographic interviews. This reveals that they aspire to be comic book collectors, feel relatively isolated in their love of comic books among their friends, and are big fans of three well-known Boston comic book authors.

Now here is where it finally gets interesting!

Using this data, you can craft an outreach message inviting them to join a community and find other comic book lovers.

You can tell them you're creating a unique group just for Bostonites in the community; a place where they can share their collections, arrange meet-ups, and find others just like them.

But getting them to join the community isn't enough. You can schedule interviews with comic book bigwigs and invite those in Boston to submit their questions. This gets them not only to visit the community but to actually participate as well.

OPTIMIZING THE CONVERSION PROCESS

If the process of growing the community were as described above, communities would be far easier to build. Unfortunately, people are fickle. It's relatively easy to get someone to participate in the community, even two or three times; it's far harder to convert them to a regular, active, member of the community.

It's common for most people to drop out after visiting the community but before becoming a regular member. In fact, the number of regular members compared with new visitors is usually miniscule. For many, this presents a frustrating problem. For data-driven community managers, like you (!), it presents a terrific opportunity.

You need to analyze the newcomer to regular member conversion funnel, pinpoint where members are dropping out, and then use proven theory to improve the ratio of newcomers who become regulars.

I've outlined the five stages of conversion on the following page. It begins with the first visit, then registration, participation, becoming a regular, and volunteering.

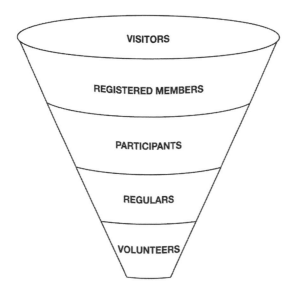

Conversion Funnel

STAGE 1: PROMOTIONAL EFFORTS TO OUTREACH

How many visitors are your promotional efforts attracting to the community platform? If you've been working hard to get bloggers/journalists to write about your community and send traffic your way, you should then be able to see how many visitors each media outlet sent.

To measure this top-line figure, use the number of unique new visitors per month via Google Analytics. This involves multiplying the number of unique visitors per month by the percentage of new visits as shown on the following page:

# Visitors Overview			
# 20110401-20120430			
# ----------------------------------			
Month	**Unique Visitors**	**% New Visits**	**Unique new visitors**
0	21,639	66.13%	14310
1	18,454	63.79%	11772
2	20,726	64.64%	13397
3	22,884	67.60%	15470
4	24,183	69.34%	16768
5	25,088	71.49%	17935
6	25,656	71.59%	18367
7	27,146	71.53%	19418
8	29,048	71.45%	20755
9	32,465	70.41%	22859
10	33,249	62.00%	20614
11	32,496	58.39%	18974
12	32,977	58.36%	19245
Total	**346,011**	**66.16%**	**228921**

Visitor numbers

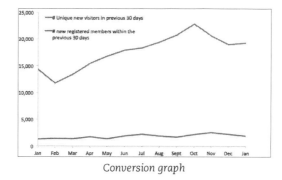

Conversion graph

This data shows a general increase in the number of unique new visitors within the previous 30 days.

You use unique new visitors for several reasons. First, unique visitors are the number of unique IP addresses that have visited your site. This excludes a single person visiting multiple times (at least from the same IP address). Second, you assume that returning visitors are generally members (not always true, but highly likely). You want to know the number of individuals that are likely to register for the community during this time.

Improving the number of unique, new, visitors

To improve the number of unique, new, visitors, identify what sources of traffic have or haven't worked well. Then spend more time working on good sources of traffic. If one blogger sent you twice as much traffic as others, you might want to spend more time building a closer relationship with that blogger.

You also need to differentiate between the different channels of growth: direct growth (targeting people with whom you have existing contacts/relationships), word-of-mouth growth (mentions by members/sharing content on various platforms), promotional growth, search and other sources.

Imagine, for example, if you directly invite members to join a community. You invite your Facebook fans or Twitter followers to join. You can identify which unique channel works best. And, even within that channel, you can identify which specific type of message works best.

Head spinning? Let's break it down.

YOUR PLATFORM HAD 275,000 VISITORS WITHIN THE LAST MONTH.
- 80,000 of them came via search.
- 100,000 of them came via Facebook/Twitter.
- 50,000 of them came via word-of-mouth activities.
- The rest came from a variety of smaller channels.

Within social media platforms of your existing audiences, you see that 80,000 came via Facebook and 20,000 via Twitter.

Within that Facebook list, you can cross-reference when visitors visited (the average link on Facebook lasts a matter of hours) and see which messages were most effective. For example, did most people visit when you published a specific link or post in a particular style? Is there a pattern there? Remember that you want to know about *statistical significance*.

So a change of 1% to 5% doesn't matter much unless it's over a sustained period of time, but a change of 40% is something you want to pay attention to.

You want to identify within each channel which specific messages lead to growth. When you know this, you can optimize these messages. You can identify a balance that will optimize the number of visitors to the community platform and shift your own efforts to match this.

Unfortunately, it gets a little more complicated. Not all visitors are created equal. Search traffic, for example, is likely to result in fewer registered members than directly inviting your friends to visit and join the community. Instead of just tracking the number of visitors to a community platform, you need to identify the conversion ratio of visitors to registered members.

So, you want to know not only sources of growth to traffic, but also which sources lead to registered members. Using Google Analytics, you can identify that. You browse where visitors visit from and where they go once they arrive. How many click on the link to register? How many who register actually complete the registration process?

Key metrics:
- Unique visits per traffic source per 30 days compared with the previous 30 days.
- Registrations per traffic source per 30 days compared with the previous 30 days.

- Activities within each traffic source that led to membership growth.

Possible interventions

The standard intervention at this level is to try multiple channels of growth. There are four channels for growing a community:

1. **Direct recruitment of people you already have some connection with.** For example, your mailing lists, social media followers/fans, and other existing contacts. Data may be collected both from community analytics and mailing list data (usually the number of people who clicked the link to visit the community). Be aware that some platforms, such as Twitter, aren't easy to track because many hits appear as direct traffic. So you need to specifically measure this by the bit.ly clicks or by measuring the increased visits within the hour after that tweet was published.

2. **Word of mouth/referrals is your existing audience mentioning the community to others.** This may be extremely difficult to measure without a clear program/link for encouraging referrals. However, it's not impossible to put together a rough estimation. This will include increased direct visits during the period of significant WOM/referral activities, visits to specific pages set up for this activity, and traffic from Facebook/Twitter sharing (from members, as opposed to you).

3. **Promotion is gaining coverage in external channels where your target audience tends to congregate.** Don't try to measure every single piece of coverage; work backwards from those who Google Analytics shows as delivering a good source of traffic. If you aren't measuring direct visitors, then measure the increase in visitors during the period of that promotional activity. This includes mentions in popular groups, coverage in top news sites and invitations to mailing lists.

   - Try multiple promotional techniques. For example, host a live chat with a popular person of influence and encourage them to mention it to their audience.

- Build relationships with popular bloggers. This includes mentions in popular groups, coverage in top news sites and invitations to mailing lists.

4. Search/miscellaneous traffic can be measured directly by almost any platform analytics package.

STAGE 2: VISITORS TO REGISTERED MEMBERS

Once you have optimized the number of visitors to your community, you need to increase the number of those visitors that register to become members. First, however, you need to identify this figure.

Measuring visitors to registered members

Compare the number of newly registered members within the previous 30 days (or month) with the number of registrations during the same period. Google Analytics doesn't show the number of registrations unless members are taken to a registration-complete page.

To get the number of new registrations, you probably need to either individually list members by the date they joined and find out how many joined during any given month, or use a platform that has a statistics package that shows you how many members joined during the previous month.

Visitor to registered member conversion	Jan	Feb	Mar	Apr	May	Jun	Jul
# Unique new visitors in previous 30 days	14,310	11,772	13,397	15,470	16,768	17,935	18,
# new registered members within the previous 30 days	1306	1411	1377	1725	1372	1898	2
Registration conversion %	9.13%	11.99%	10.28%	11.15%	8.18%	10.58%	12.0

Visitors to newcomers

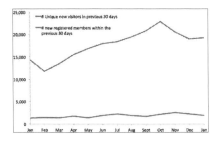

This graph shows that even though the number of unique new visitors has risen, the number of newly registered members has not increased at the same pace: a clear loss of potential members.

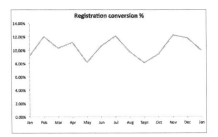

A single graph shows the ups and down of the registration conversion percentage.

Optimizing the newcomer to registration conversion ratio

To highlight exactly where you can increase this ratio, you need to break the registration down into a series of steps you expect members to take.

A typical process for a newcomer to become a member is:

- Step 1) Visits (unique new visitors)
- Step 2) Identifies something interesting to respond to/ participate in
- Step 3) Clicks to register
- Step 4) Completes registration form
- Step 5) Opens confirmation e-mail
- Step 6) Clicks the link to confirm registration

At the moment the only data points you have are at the two opposite ends; you need data throughout this process. By tracking the number of members that click the registration link, the number that complete the registration form, the e-mail open-rates (where available), and the clicks to confirm the registration, you gain the necessary data.

For example:

Visitor to registered member conversion												
# Unique new visitors in previous 30 days	14,310	11,772	13,397	15,470	16,768	17,935	18,367	19,418	20,755	22,859	20,614	18,974	19,245
# visitors to registration page	4293	3675	4005	4785	5143	5229	5512	5972	6413	663	5992	5630	5471
# completed registration form	2999	2674	2903	3558	3600	3993	3689	4057	4138	4641	4203	3845	3709
# opened confirmation e-mail	1789	1704	1741	2235	2060	2195	2655	2431	2282	2574	2907	2702	2238
# clicked confirmation e-mail link	1431	1494	1392	1958	1894	1902	2496	2084	1901	2307	2730	2507	1995
# new registered members within the pre	1306	1411	1377	1725	1372	1898	2219	1890	1681	2152	2520	2238	1907
Registration conversion %	9.13%	11.99%	10.28%	11.15%	8.18%	10.58%	12.08%	9.73%	8.10%	9.41%	12.22%	11.80%	9.91%

Visitors to registered members conversion

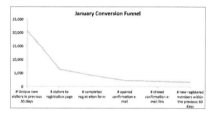

This analysis is solely for the most recent month.

You can now identify specifically where members are dropping out and design interventions to improve this ratio. The biggest win in the graph above would be from unique new visitors in the previous 30 days to clicks to the registration page.

Increasing clicks on registration page

There are several ways to improve clicks on the registration page.

- **Target more interested members.** The biggest influence upon the likelihood of a newcomer becoming a regular member is their strength of interest in the topic. If you take extra care to only invite from pools of people with an above-average level of interest in the topic, it should be easier to convert them into regular members of the community.

- **Tweak the positioning of registration.** You don't want registration to appear in big, flickering, lights at the top of every page. You do, however, need it to be prominently positioned on the website.

BackYard Chickens

- **Position the latest activity above the fold.** The fold is a term from when newspapers were delivered to customers folded. Stories positioned above the fold would receive far more attention. Today, it also refers to the area of the website you can see before scrolling down. Don't waste valuable real estate on a large graphic; show the latest activity above the fold on the homepage of the community.

Lenovo shows the latest activity above the fold on their homepage for the community.

- **Use a prompt to register.** After members have clicked (x) pages on the community, they are prompted to register. They become engaged in the community before being invited to join and respond to a discussion.

Increasing completion of the registration form

Once members have clicked on the registration form, your conversion rate should be extremely high. Keep the amount of data you require at an absolute minimum. Anything more than their desired username, e-mail, and password is irrelevant at this stage.

- **Let members create their first contribution, then prompt the member to register.** This is slightly different from what I suggest above. Instead of prompting members to register after they visit (x) pages, this allows members to create their first post to the community (usually in response to a discussion) and then prompt them to register. Technically more difficult to execute, this approach is more likely to motivate newcomers to complete the registration process to avoid losing the post they already created.

- **Reduce the copy required to complete the registration form.** Many registration forms ask for copious amounts of irrelevant information. The form to join GenerationBenz.com continues for six pages. The registration form to join the Camden community in London even asked members personal questions such as their sexuality. None of this is necessary. All you need at this stage is a login name, an e-mail address, and a password.

Spreedly signup

- **Change the tone of copy.** Some community platforms do not allow you to use a simplified version of a form as shown above. Instead, you might need to tweak the copy to encourage a registration. This may include highlighting existing members, benefits of the community, or activities members can participate in once they have joined.

- **Tweak the design of the form.** You can also tweak the color, size, and layout of the registration form. Avoid being too clever. It's better to stay simple.

- **Use Facebook/OpenID registration.** Another option is to allow members to register via accounts on other platforms, e.g. Twitter, Facebook, or OpenID.

Increasing opens of the confirmation e-mail

A surprisingly large number of members are typically lost between completing the registration form and opening the confirmation e-mail. To ensure better rates of confirmation e-mail opening, try the following:

- **Change the 'from' address.** Some people instinctively don't open e-mails from organizations. Try using the community manager's name to send the e-mail (as opposed to the name of the community).

- **Increase the speed the confirmation e-mail is sent.** Anything longer than a minute is a failure. Members want to participate straight away. If they don't get an e-mail for 30 minutes, a few hours, or even a few days (!), then you're almost certain to lose the member. The sooner the confirmation is sent, the better.

- **Change the subject line.** It is worthwhile testing several different subject lines to find the one that is best suited to your community. You might find, for example, that "(community name) new member confirmation" isn't as engaging as "30 minutes until your brand new account self-destructs."

- **Run a spam filter check.** If the ratio here is extremely low, do a spam filter check. Most e-mail platforms now allow you to do this. They test the spam filters with the major account providers to see if it's likely to end up in the spam folder. If this happens, keep tweaking and changing until it doesn't.

Increasing clicks on confirmation e-mail link

Next you want people to click the confirmation link. The conversion rate at this stage is usually high, but could be higher. There are again some tweaks you can make within the body of the e-mail itself that can increase your ratio. These include:

- **Reduce the quantity of copy.** Confirmation e-mails rarely need more than a single link explaining the recipient has to click the link below.

- **Highlight a specific action to take (or bonus for clicking the link).** In the rare scenario when reducing the quantity of copy hasn't had a big impact, try highlighting a specific action members can take within the community (once they have clicked the link). This should usually be to participate in a topical interaction.

The results of these interventions will vary by community.

You should have a regular process for benchmarking, testing interventions, and then adapting to what works best. Optimizing is an ongoing process, not a single event.

STAGE 3: REGISTERED MEMBERS TO PARTICIPANTS

Now you have increased the number of members that register for the community, you want to ensure they participate. A member who doesn't participate is a lurker, and lurkers hold very little value to the community.

This metric is relatively simple. You look at the number of new people who have completed the registration process in the data and compare it with the number that have made a contribution.

If this figure isn't immediately apparent in your data (Google Analytics won't track this), then you may need to use a surveying technique. You might need to use systematic sampling of 100 to 200 members (this picks a member per every Nth (e.g. 10) that joined as listed by date—relevant due to the likelihood of older members being more likely to have made a contribution than those who joined yesterday). Of these 100 to 200 members, how many made a contribution?

How does this compare to last month? If they didn't make a contribution, why didn't they make a contribution? What could be done to improve this figure? Again, you want to look at the trends per month and identify if this figure is improving, getting worse, or has remained relatively flat.

For example:

Registered member to participants	Jan	Feb	Mar	Apr	May	Jun	Jul	Aug	Sept	Oct	Nov	Dec	Jan
Members sampled	32	107	54	74	84	84	72	71	101	103	78	84	91
Members whom made a contribution	11	17	18	12	24	29	25	25	32	33	30	25	38
% of members whom made a contribution	34%	16%	33%	16%	29%	35%	35%	35%	32%	32%	38%	30%	42%
Est. no. members made a contribution	449	224	459	280	392	655	770	665	533	689	969	666	796

Registered members to participants

Here are sampled members who joined in the previous month and how many of them made a contribution then to the community. This gives you a percentage figure, to multiply by the number of registrations during that period for an estimated number of members that made a contribution.

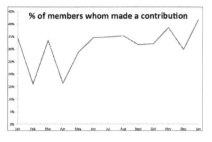

% of members contribution

Here are ways to convert more newly registered members into active participants:

- **Change the post-registration page.** After clicking the confirmation link, don't send newcomers to the homepage. Instead send them to a page that highlights something they can participate in straight away. This should be a topical discussion, poll, or registration for an upcoming event/ activity. Solicit that first contribution as soon as possible.

- **Change the welcome e-mail.** Change the e-mail sent after the confirmation link is sent. Keep this welcome e-mail short and highlight a discussion that you want members to contribute to. You can update with a new discussion every week.

- **Create a newcomer area.** Create a specific, visible, newcomer area in the community, which explains the basics, and how newcomers can get involved. Make this a visible link from the homepage of the community.

- **Reminders to participate.** If newcomers have joined but haven't made a contribution, schedule an automated reminder highlight saying you're sorry about that and offer something they can do in the community.

- **Personal welcomes (and types of welcome).** In the early stages of the community, you might also personally welcome members. If a personal welcome does get a member to participate over a long period of time compared with other methods, you should keep doing them. Otherwise, stop doing them. Your time is limited; how you spend it matters.

STAGE 4: PARTICIPANTS TO LONG-TERM MEMBERS

Now it becomes more complicated. You want to know how many first-time participants become long-term members. Long-term members are defined as still active after six months.

The only way to get this data is to sample those who participated six months ago and compare that number with the number of those still participating today. Again, you can't sample all members.

It's a multi-stage process, because you want to know specifically when members drop out. The more specific you can be, the better you can design an intervention to help. You want to know what activity stage members tend to drop out (e.g. after the first contribution, second contribution, fifth contribution) and when members tend to vanish (e.g. after one day, one week, one month, six months).

Both are important. The activity stage indicates what activity hurdle members need to jump to become regular members. The time stage indicates the point after which the community begins to become a habit for members.

For example, it's common for communities to attract people who participate heavily for a very short duration of time and then get bored and vanish. At a pure data level, this might make you think you need to plan an intervention after the 25th contribution as opposed to simply finding a way to get a member to stay after the second week.

With some of our clients, for example, we often find members make a single contribution but then never return. This might be because they forget about the community. Visiting the community never becomes a habit as it does with, say, Facebook or Twitter.

It might be because the notification system is awful and members never learn when people reply to their contribution and, thus, have no reason to return. If you make a contribution, leave the community and never hear back, you will probably never visit the community again. Even a minor change in this area, such as changing the notification system from opt-in to opt-out, can have a staggering impact upon the conversion ratio.

Brett Taylor, founder of Friendfeed and former CTO of Facebook, noted that his data showed that if members befriended five individuals on the platform, they would likely become permanent members of the community. This is true of most online communities (five is not necessarily *the* number but *a* number exists for your community).

Once Brett knew his number, he could plan interventions that would encourage members to befriend five people on the platform: finding people that members knew via Gmail/Facebook integration, introducing members to members like them, automatically entering them into groups based upon details listed in their profile pages or hosting newcomer-related activities that would force people to interact with each other.

Unless you're collecting data along both activity *and* duration of membership paths, you won't be able to pinpoint what sort of intervention you need to plan.

Measuring the participants to regulars

In an ideal world, it helps to have a data package built in to the community platform. However, for many of you, this won't be an option. Alternatively, you can use 100 members in the *systematic sampling* method described on page 75.

Divide the group into active/non-active members. Then, within the dropout group, identify where they dropped out. Place them in different categories. First contribution to second, second to third, third to fifth, fifth to tenth, etc.

Months since joining	1	2	3	4	5	6
Members	57	37	21	19	19	15
% decrease		35%	43%	10%	0%	21%
Contributions since joining	1 to 5	6 to 10	11 to 15	16 to 20	21 to 25	26 to 30
Members	100	47	31	24	11	8
% decrease		53%	34%	23%	54%	27%

Months and contributions since joining

The table above shows the latest figures available. You see that a sample of 100, which made a contribution six months ago, was used for the time duration. Of these, 37 were still active after two months, 21 were still active after three months, 19 were still active after four months, 19 still active after five months and 15 still active after six months.

Below, I have used a sample of 100 members who made a single contribution six months ago to identify where they dropped out: 47 made six or more contributions, 31 made 11 or more contributions, 24 made one or more contributions, 11 made 21 or more contributions and just eight made more than 26 contributions.

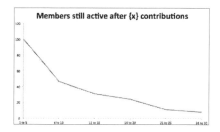

Members active after contributions

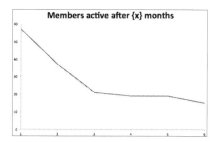

Members active after {x} months

You can see that the number of members that leave after three months is relatively low compared to the first three months. You might plan a series of activities to keep a newcomer engaged for the first three months.

Let's use another example. Imagine that you notice members are vanishing after the third week. You might plan a ritual or some sort of graduation for members every third week of the month. You might write a post that mentions members by name, has a few details about them, and gives them access to specific forums within the community platform.

You also want to collect anecdotal data on what types of contributions members who became regulars in the community made compared with those who left. What was the difference? Were there particular discussions that those who became regulars participated in at each phase compared with those who didn't become members? Can you place these contributions into categories? For instance, "*self-disclosure discussions,*" "*status-jockeying discussions,*" and "*conveying information discussions.*"

You can guide newcomers into participating in the types of discussions that are likely to keep them engaged in the community. In addition, was there anything else that regulars did which those that left didn't? Did they complete their profile? Upload a picture of themselves? Submit a story? Have a discussion with a community manager?

By doing this, you should be able to see which type of discussions and activities helped members progress through each stage. Some of this is undoubtedly subjective, and part of it is sheer luck, but it should be possible to review 100 members and get a fairly good idea of what turns a newcomer into a long-term community member.

Possible interventions

- **Reminders/notifications.** You might add or tweak your notification system. The notification system should be opt-out and remind members when there is a new response to their own contributions.

- **Guide to self-disclosure discussions/status-jockeying.** Guide the newcomers into self-disclosure or status-jockeying discussions. Try to get members interacting in discussions in which they have an emotional stake and are thus likely to return frequently to see the responses to their own contributions. This helps create the habit of visiting the community.

- **Rituals/graduations.** You might use a ritual/graduation for newcomers after they have made a certain number of contributions or been an active member for a certain period of time. This might be increased levels of access to the community, a detailed sheet of inside jokes, mentions in news posts, or a listing in the community history for that month.

- **Buddy systems.** In mature communities, you may have an insider group or base of volunteers with whom you can develop a buddy system—members take responsibility for building relationships with newcomers and keep them active and happy within the community for the first few months.

- **Web reputation system.** For mature communities, you can add web reputation systems, scoring/ranking systems that make an individual's implicit reputation explicit. This motivates newcomers to increase their standing and existing members to continue participating to maintain their standing.

- **Events/activities.** You might develop a series of events for newcomers to participate in—quizzes, beginner-level guides to the topics, or even in-person meetings for newcomers.

- **Newcomer threads/forums.** In addition to newcomer threads and forums, you might also initiate threads solely for newcomers to ask questions regulars might consider basic (or even dumb). You might also write content about newcomers.

- **Cultural education.** You can ensure newcomers get quality, positive, responses from their early contributions. Research shows that the initial response to a member's first post is a major factor in whether the user will make a second response.

- **Provide ownership opportunities.** One method to keep members engaged beyond the initial burst of enthusiasm is to facilitate opportunities for members to take ownership over areas of the site by writing a regular column for the community, conducting interviews, taking responsibility for responding to certain discussion topics. This should only be enabled after (x) months of membership, or after (x) contributions to the community (the figure should vary depending upon when members are dropping out of the community).

You can extend this process further, say from six months to a year, from members who make five contributions a month to those who make 50. Just remember that the goal is optimization of the process and, as I have said, optimization of your own time to achieve the best possible results for your community.

Beyond a certain point, further optimization of the process won't be the best use of your time. The secret is to find that sweet spot.

STAGE 5: LONG-TERM MEMBERS TO VOLUNTEERS

If you work on the assumption that every member could become a volunteer for your community, then it's worthwhile tracking how many *do* become volunteers.

Community volunteers are the most effective means of scaling the online community. Community volunteers can take on a variety of roles: initiating and responding to discussions, inviting people to join the community, creating content, keeping members engaged, moderating discussions, promoting the community externally, hosting activities/events for the community and collecting/analyzing data.

As the community manager's time is limited, recruiting volunteers provides the most scalable method of doing more with the same amount of time. Recruiting a number of volunteers should be an integral and ongoing part of the community manager's role—and certainly one worth tracking.

Keep in mind that the number of community members who become volunteers will be low; almost certainly in the low single-percentage digits compared to the number of members in the community. This is not a cause for alarm, but rather an opportunity.

By increasing the number of volunteers you can significantly increase the level of growth, activity, and sense of community. Your role shifts from managing members to managing volunteers. You can get far more done. You can increase the overall energy of the community. It's not all you now, it's a diverse collection of people running the community.

How we gather this data

This is the easiest data to gather; look at the number of regular members in the community and the number of listed volunteers. In most communities, the community manager knows the volunteers personally. In larger communities, it should be possible to list members by their access level within the community platform (e.g. 128 members have level 2 access).

The key metric isn't the absolute number of volunteers (although that can be interesting) but rather the number of volunteers to the absolute number of active members. You want to know the number to whom you have given advanced access levels in the community compared with the total number of returning visitors to your community (or if your platform can list the number of active members within the past month, this figure is an adequate substitute).

This will mean bringing data from two different sources into an Excel spreadsheet (and then using that spreadsheet to create a graph)—isn't data fun?

Clearly, there is a danger that a negative attribute could be construed as a positive. For example, while you want the number of volunteers to active members to be as high as possible, you shouldn't automatically assume that an increase is a good thing.

If the number of volunteers remained constant and the number of active members plummeted, you would see a sudden, sharp, rise in your ratio. Before you whoop for delight, be aware that this is terrible. It means your volunteers are either doing a bad job, or something very wrong has happened in the community. It's most likely your volunteers are failing.

On the other hand, if your volunteers do a terrific job and the number of active members in your community *increases*, the ratio would drop. This means your volunteers are doing great, but you're not recruiting enough volunteers to keep pace with the community.

It's also worthwhile tracking the volunteers-to-growth ratio, volunteers-to-activity, and volunteers-to-sense of community, all of which will provide a good indicator of how your volunteers are doing in each area.

Key metrics:
- Regular members to volunteers (advanced access levels)
- Number of volunteers to sense of community
- Number of volunteers to growth

Possible interventions
- Add a *get more involved* area. Most communities would benefit from an area within the community that would allow motivated members to get more involved.
- **Proactively seek out people who make contributions to get more involved.** If someone makes a series of outstanding contributions to a community, you might want to contact them to see if they can become a regular volunteer for your community on that topic.
- **Have volunteers coach additional volunteers.** You might get your existing volunteers to recruit and coach new volunteers. This is ideal because it takes you out of the process.
- **Headhunt volunteers.** You might also personally headhunt the members you want to become volunteers. Some might naturally show higher levels of maturity and expertise than others.
- **Host an application process.** In one of my first communities, we had an application process for volunteers. It was competitive. Members had to explain a little about

themselves, their motivation and their experience for the position. It also had the effect of gaining better volunteers.

## CHAPTER 3

Content

Many of us have the wrong idea about the role of content within an online community. You can waste a lot of time trying to create what you think is the 'best' content for your online community. Fortunately, however, there is a better way.

My first proper community management job was working for the Virtual Gamers Association. This was an organization of video game centers, where people would come to play games against each other using PCs, PlayStations, or Nintendos. For the first few months, I would spend hours every day scanning the various video game news sites and trying to write the most informative post.

Not only did it consume a lot of my time, it was demotivating and failed to provoke a big reaction from the target audience. Most of the target audience read the same news sites as I did and didn't want to wait a little longer to get the news from me (we are pretty fixed in our news-consumption habits). Worse still, it put our site in competition with the larger news sites, which we wanted to promote us.

About three months in, I was short on time and needed to get a news post up as soon as possible. One of our gaming centers had recently held a competition, so I wrote about the matches and got a quote from the winner.

Within six hours, that post had gained 37 comments (the average was one or two). The people involved in the event had participated; other gamers had chimed in with their views, and even better, one of the bigger sites had mentioned it as a snippet, which sent more traffic our way. I had stumbled across the biggest secret about community content.

From then on, nearly all my content was about the community. I did interviews with members, I wrote about upcoming events, I wrote about what members were achieving both inside and outside of the community. I let members submit their own columns and posts too. I even wrote a few gossip columns (trust me, be careful with that).

The result was instant. Members began visiting every day to see if they or their friends had been mentioned. This site became the local newspaper for my community. Our members spent a lot of time responding to discussions. The number of return visits and activity skyrocketed.

This brings us to the fundamental rule of community content:

THE BEST CONTENT FOR A COMMUNITY IS CONTENT ABOUT THE COMMUNITY

The role of content is not to provide the latest information. That's a cutthroat business that will take up a lot of your time and (even if you are able to succeed, which is tough), won't produce big results. The role of content is not even to inform individuals about the subject or the organization.

Content about the topic or the organization encourages people to read and not participate. You're creating a content site instead of a community.

Think of your content as the equivalent of a local community newspaper that tells you what's going on in the local community. The content area of an online community is the same. It tells you what's happening in the local online community.

This means you need to make it about people *in* the community.

The role of the community newspaper

As modern communities become increasingly large and diverse, people use the local community newspaper to integrate themselves into smaller, more homogenous communities.

As the internet becomes a busier, anonymous, place, people need 'local newspapers' to integrate themselves into groups of individuals. Local newspapers help individuals to feel a sense of belonging and attachment to a group of likeminded people.

Individuals judge the importance of all but the very largest news stories by its impact upon their group. While events such as 9/11 are considered important by all within the country and around the world simply via its unsurpassed coverage, any less major stories will be given different levels of importance depending upon the impact they have upon the local communities.

However, people need a narrative to gauge the impact such news has upon their community. The local newspaper performs a key role as a facilitating agent for the community, including building consensus, highlighting conflict, and providing a reference group for others in the community.

Establishing a social order and narrative

Newspapers also perform less-deliberate roles. For example, newspapers (and all media) also establish a social order among individuals within the community. Those who are frequently mentioned are considered important and worthy of constant coverage. These individuals are at the top of the social ladder. Those who are never mentioned rank towards the bottom of the social ladder.

Individuals who undertake noteworthy activities or are involved in significant events will receive increasing levels of attention. While this may merit negative as much as positive attention, it still provides an effective motivation for soliciting positive contributions to a community.

The joy of a local newspaper is any individual can be mentioned for any remarkable action. Readers never know when they will find friends, colleagues, acquaintances and family mentioned in the paper. They also know that there is a high probability that they, too, are likely to one day be featured in the newspaper.

The local newspaper puts the many different facets of a community into a narrative and sets the agenda. The newspaper establishes which news and people are most important. It creates a consensus around the community and provides the means for individuals to be able to follow the *ongoing story* of the community.

Inform and entertain

Community newspapers do provide a range of relevant information, from upcoming events and job advertisements to the latest topical news and a summary of what has recently taken place within the community.

For example, if you have a community event coming up, that would merit attention (it doesn't even have to be your event—just an event that will be of interest to members).

A community newspaper will also provide entertainment. This may include guest columns, gossip, interviews, reviews, previews and other elements most commonly associated with newspapers. The entertainment value of newspapers is not to be underestimated. Newspapers without such content struggle to achieve and sustain high levels of readership.

Social

Finally, a local newspaper tells the local community what to think about issues. Many people struggle to make up their mind, even when they have personal experience with the issue. They seek out the opinions of others and try to be on the right side of the community majority.

The community newspaper is both the consensus of community opinion and the determinant for the community's opinion. While this may appear subversive, such a role is beneficial to a community. It provides a community with a shared emotional connection, which is vital for a strong sense of community.

Local newspapers play a major role in the success of communities. I believe that online communities need a similar newspaper element. Like many thriving hyperlocal communities today, a community needs a newspaper that is focused on telling the stories of people in the community.

Such an online newspaper will provide information for members, establish a social order and facilitate strong bonds and heightened sense of community. Online community managers should look to local community newspapers for content inspiration and avoid getting drawn into the *industry news* trap.

So the goal of content is:

- **Creates a narrative for the community to allow members to follow what's happening.** If they miss a few days, they can read the content to catch up.

- **Provides a reason for members to visit the community every day or frequently.** They can see if they or their friends have been mentioned.

- **Develops a sense of community among members.** It provides a unique identity. Members get to learn more about other people like them. They feel they are going through an experience as part of a group as opposed to being alone.

- **Establishes a social order among the community and highlights the top members.** This social order challenges people to continually participate positively in the community to maintain or increase their status.

- **Subtly influences the community by emphasizing activities that you wish to encourage.** If you want more members participating in a specific discussion, you can write content about that discussion.

PRINCIPLES OF GREAT CONTENT

Initiate discussions and activities

The catch of making the content about the community is you need things in the community to write about. This often means you need to initiate those things. You might, for example, initiate a discussion within the community and then write a news post about the discussion.

Or you might initiate and write about an event (see the events and activities section on page 163). If you're short on inspiration, you can pick up a local newspaper and see the types of stories they write about.

Use a consistent tone of voice and frequency

The content of the community should be written in a voice that reflects the personalities of members in the community as reflected in your audience analysis. This tone of voice may be caring, sardonic, sarcastic, casual, laid back, formal or a cross between several categories. Try to avoid the content sounding like a corporate press release.

Content must also be published at a regular frequency. For most online communities, content will be posted daily. Don't make three posts one day and then be absent for a few days.

There are many types of content. Each type falls within a category such as interviews. The community manager needs to identify what categories are most popular and then specifically which elements within the category are most popular.

Mention people by name

Community content must mention names of people in the community in up to 90% of stories. If you read any local newspaper, you will overwhelmingly see stories that mention people by name. In fact, local newspapers know to cram as many mentions of people in the community as possible.

They do this because they know that the more names mentioned, the more people are likely to read the newspaper to see if they or people they know are mentioned. Mentioning names of individuals affected by the news or writing about specific people increases readership of the content considerably and enhances the sense of community among members.

Mentioning names also spotlights members, which helps encourage desired behavior and develop a social order among members. A social order is required for individuals to compare themselves against each other. A social order provides people with icons they aspire to be and a means of tracking progress vis-à-vis those to whom they feel superior.

Aspiration and spotlighting

Members who are frequently featured in community content are quickly established at the top of the community's social ladder. This will usually be those who have made the best contributions, made the most contributions or have some other unique attribute that distinguishes them from other community members.

They are, essentially, being rewarded for their contributions with increased visibility and status. By showcasing these individuals, you're inviting others to also make quality contributions so they too can be *spotlighted.*

These individuals become the reference point toward which others aspire. You can see this effect in celebrity and fashion magazines. Readers aspire to imitate various aspects, from hairstyles, to fashion, to achievements and even the negative behavior of the celebrities featured in these magazines

You should use content to give individuals who have made contributions that you want others to emulate a high level of exposure. This spotlighting (showering attention upon specific people) is one of the key influences a community manager retains over the community.

The clear challenge is determining which members deserve to be spotlighted in the community.

Developing a recognition criteria

A criterion for recognition is a set of rules that determine which individuals to spotlight. In some communities, this will be determined by a reputation system rather than subjective judgments.

This criterion may include:

- **Excellent contribution.** A user who makes an outstanding contribution to the community should be featured.
- **Number of contributions.** A member who has made a certain number of contributions within the community might be regularly mentioned within news posts, interviews and other types of content.
- **Veteran members.** Members who have been registered for a long period of time may be mentioned more frequently than newcomers. This rewards those who have registered early and ensures veterans don't feel 'crowded out' by newcomers.

- **Expertise in a specific area.** Members who have high levels of expertise in a particular area may be mentioned in reference to such fields.

- **Newcomers.** It is useful to mention some newcomers to the community. This is likely to increase goodwill towards newcomers and help newcomers become emotionally invested in the success of the community.

- **Subjective.** It is also useful for the community manager to have both subjective and ad-hoc reasons for giving attention to members. For example, the community manager might decide to spotlight a member with a unique personality or in a remarkable circumstance.

Using data, you can track quality contributions, the number of contributions, or a number of *good* contributions within a specific area.

Your criterion will not be a static set of rules but a continuous development. As members contribute news posts, have been members for longer and have made increasingly outstanding contributions, the spotlight bar will continue to rise.

THE SOCIAL ORDER DEBATE

Content establishes a social order that encourages both aspiration and a sense of superiority over those below. Although this sense of superiority may seem negative, it performs a fundamental role in retaining members.

A sense of superiority over others is a way of retaining members and helping members judge where they stand within a community. It may sound manipulative and conniving; certainly I've seen some people push back on this. Yet this process helps the community in the long run. All social groups need some form of social order to function.

Members need to compare themselves against each other. If they only see those standing higher, they might decide that the social ladder is impossible to climb within this community. By being able to gate their progress either up or down the ladder they are *more* likely to participate.

CONTENT CATEGORIES

A broad variety of content may be used for an online community, including the following:

News

News is the key source of content and primarily features what is happening within the community.

There are two types of news: news about the community and news about the community's broader ecosystem. Community news covers updates that may include:

- **Latest events.** Organized both inside and outside of the community, these events can include challenges, competitions, online live-chats, offline meet-ups and broader events taking place within the ecosystem.

- **New members.** News posts might be used to welcome new members and help convert these members into regular participants.

- **Latest/most popular discussions.** News can highlight the latest and most popular discussions taking place within the community, including links to where people can participate.

- **Member contributions.** News articles written by members or excellent pieces of advice and insights for other members.

- **News about members.** News about members of the community might include their latest achievements such as having a child, getting married, being promoted to a new job/starting their own business.

- **Update on a relevant issue.** If the community is fundraising or participating in a specific cause, it should provide regular updates to members of the community.

Announcements

Similar to news, the content will periodically include announce-ments from the company or about the community highlighting some major news or change that will impact members of the community. An announcement might, for example, be the launch of a new sub-group within the community or a call for volunteers to participate in the community.

Feature articles

Community content should include more in-depth feature articles such as:

- **Interviews.** Interviews should be a regular feature to shine an immediate spotlight upon members of the community. These interviews may be with either members of the community, those from the organization, or VIPs from within the community's ecosystem.
- **Analysis.** Content may include in-depth analysis on relevant issues within the community. Issues ideally should be based upon data and evidence.
- **Stories/articles.** Major sources of articles are stories about members of the community and information articles on an interesting topic. Stories might involve how members became interested in the community, what other members think of the subjects and their achievements. Articles can concern any topic that the community might have an interest in. This might be a profile of a relevant company or individual, an overview of a major issue or a narrow focus on something specific.
- **Surveys.** A community may undertake a survey and collect research that it can later publish as a feature article.
- **Reviews/previews.** The community may publish reviews or previews of upcoming events, products, services or happenings within the ecosystem.

Opinion/guest columns

- **Thoughts.** Members of the community, the community manager or people within the organization may write thought posts on their passions. This should rotate between different people to sustain a high level of interest. Members who contribute consistently good ideas should be invited to provide a weekly column for the community.

- **Predictions.** The community manager or others may create prediction posts about an upcoming topic. Or, better, the community manager may ask 10 to 20 community members to make predictions on a topical relevant issue. These predictions can then be presented as a single feature.

Classifieds

- **Jobs.** A community might have regular content about jobs within the sector and people on the move within that organization's sector. The jobs section can also highlight companies that are hiring.

- **Buying/Selling.** The content might also include members who are trading items in the community in a weekly or monthly round-up.

Promotions and advertisements

- **A community may periodically offer a promotion for members that is paid for by the advertiser or the organization.** An article can then cover the winner's experiences.

Statements from the community

An online community must assert itself within its ecosystem. It needs both its members and other individuals within the ecosystem to appreciate its rising status as an influential player.

One popular source of content, therefore, will be regular statements from the community on topical issues. These should be quickly written by a small group and put to the community for feedback within a few hours. This content should then be submitted to media publications in the sector.

Miscellaneous

A variety of other potential sources of content do not fit any of the categories above. These include content in different formats (videos, pictures, live-blogs, etc.) and uncommon content, such as a member of the year or collaborative statements.

User-generated content

It is essential that members have the opportunity to contribute content to the community. This allows them to feel a genuine sense of influence over the community and reduces the workload for the community manager. User-generated content will come via a regular core group of volunteers and through single contributions.

Communities should allow members to submit news (for approval), interviews, information about events, tip-offs, gossip and anything that may be construed as relevant to the community. The community manager may then either approve the topic, edit the article so it's suited for approval (and appears under the name of the member who submitted the article) or decide not to publish but thank the contributor and explain why it is not suitable.

User-generated content (excluding discussions) might also include photos and videos taken by the community managers or links to articles that a member feels others should read. The community needs an option or a channel through which members can submit this news.

CATEGORY REPETITION

Media channels have long embraced category repetition as a means for their content strategies. Category repetition reduces the workload, sets expectations and is finely targeted at a specific audience. The categories of content used for *Time* magazine and the *National Enquirer* are very different, for example.

Category repetition means that categories of content are repeated in every edition. A monthly magazine, for example, will frequently use a similar layout with very similar content. This content may include a combination of news articles followed by an exclusive interview, upcoming events, letters from readers, an exclusive preview/review, and a jobs section. These same categories will be present in every issue with only small alterations.

Category repetition trains the audience what to expect in each issue. Audiences expect and want familiarity in content. We also see this pattern in many television or radio shows, in which the content changes, but the categories of content remain relatively unchanged for months, or possibly years.

How many viewers/buyers of TV shows, magazines and newspapers would continue to purchase if they had little idea of what to expect? Category repetition provides the structure for the medium. The success of such a magazine/radio show/program depends as much upon the categories of content it uses as it does upon the content itself.

By embracing category repetition, these publications are also able to plan many months of content in advance and ensure they have the resources to produce such content by the required date.

Category repetition within the community

A community manager should also embrace category repetition. Such repetition provides members with a sense of stability in the community while also providing a motivation to return to see what's new. Category repetition is a useful tool for recruiting volunteers and stimulating excitement about an upcoming event or activity in the community.

Category repetition ensures that infrequent events, genuine exclusives and other unique activities receive more interest. This content stands out among the usual categories and thus attracts more attention compared with categories that are used randomly or interchangeably.

Identifying the content categories

You must identify the categories of content you will consistently use within the community. Initially these may be based upon intuition, experience, elements that have worked in other communities within the community's broader ecosystem or by audience and sector analysis data indicating a preference for certain types of content.

Content categories most likely will include news articles, interviews, a regular feature series and either jobs, gossip, classifieds or opinion columns. As you recall, there are several sub-categories within each that the community manager may specifically adopt. You may also *rotate* categories based upon set interval periods.

Each category of content should be both quantitatively and qualitatively measured. The quantitative measurements include click-throughs, page views, average time on site and return visitors. From this data, the community manager will, over a period of several months, be able to isolate the most popular categories of content and make recommendations about what should be included in the future.

Qualitative data includes what appears in the comments, whether the content is mentioned elsewhere, and what impact the content appears to have had upon the community.

Rotation

With the exception of news about the community, content categories should be rotated after significant lengths of time to keep the format fresh. Repeating the same category for an extended period of time leads to both poor writing and less exciting material.

For example, the most exciting people to interview may already have been interviewed within the first few months. Or the best opinion column topics are likely to have been covered after six months.

When the content is rotated, the community manager is able to test out new ideas and allow, for example, new VIPs within the ecosystem to emerge or new topics to arise. Previously popular categories can later be reinstated.

The community manager should create a content calendar, use regular content series and encourage contributions from other members. Content should not be overly time-consuming to write. A short news post about activities taking place in the community is better than trying to get the latest news before anyone else.

Develop a content calendar

Many community managers fall victim to reactivity. As the community grows, urgent issues increasingly take priority over the community manager's work. Time spent on initiating activities, building relationships, recruiting members and creating content gradually diminishes in favor of responding to the urgent issues of the day.

However, these seemingly urgent issues are simply the most visible (such as an argument) as opposed to the most critical to community development.

In a recent survey of community managers, around half spent the *majority* of their time resolving conflicts or removing bad content. This is common among community managers who work without a clear agenda for each day.

Without a calendar, community managers are in danger of falling in to a reactive process of managing a community and not proactively developing the community. Another benefit of a calendar is that by scheduling content on a daily basis, you are forced to create content for each day.

Establish intervals

Your content calendar will repeat its categories at a consistent interval. You need to decide how long that interval is. For example, a monthly magazine has a simple interval period of one month. Yet this varies considerably depending upon the medium. Many newspapers have an interval of a single day.

Unlike media publications whose intervals were defined by their distribution restrictions, websites can choose any interval. Intervals may be daily, weekly, bi-weekly, monthly or even annually, but you can narrow these options down through process of elimination.

Daily intervals are ill-suited to an online community. Too much content would both overwhelm members and the community management team. Annual intervals are too long a time frame. It is impractical to plan out a calendar for an entire year. This is also true for bi-annually or quarterly. So decide if your calendar intervals will be weekly, bi-weekly, or monthly.

Your choice is largely based on the size of the community. For smaller communities, the intervals are likely to be weekly. As the community grows, the calendar will be repeated bi-weekly and, later, monthly. However, unlike many of the community management principles I have covered, there are few fixed rules concerning the interval period.

Most interval periods are established as much by the organization's resources and forward planning as by characteristics of the community. Regardless of the length of the interval period set, it should remain consistent. An interval period of three months, followed by two weeks, followed by a further month will be confusing for the audience to follow and difficult to plan for.

Creating a calendar

A content calendar should identify not only the categories of content that will be used, but also the specific content that will feature within that category for that date.

You can look at both online and offline content produced within the sector to identify the most popular categories. This is easier to identify in online content by both the number of comments such categories receive and their placement upon the community platform. The inclusion of these categories is usually a good indicator in itself that they are popular with the audience.

From the categories of content listed below, identify which you will use on which days.

- News
- Announcements
- Feature articles
- Guest columns
- Classifieds
- Promotions
- Statements from the community
- Miscellaneous

For example, a calendar at a single-week interval may look like:

- **Monday:** Daily Community News + Feature interview with Mark Smith about (topic)
- **Tuesday:** Daily Community News + Opinion column from a community member (John Doe)
- **Wednesday:** Daily Community News + Promotion of live-chat about (topic)
- **Thursday:** Daily Community News + Feature interview with Jane Roddis (VIP)
- **Friday:** Promotions day (sponsors discount offer) + Welcome newcomers
- **Saturday:** Summary of the week
- **Sunday:** Preview of the week ahead

Remember that within each category are several sub-categories. News, notably, may be about the latest events, new members, new/popular discussions, unique contributions, member milestones/achievements or an update on a topical issue.

In the sample calendar above, the daily community news is a constant update of the latest activity. The other category features can be reused every week.

On a calendar with a monthly interval, categories such as newcomer of the month, member of the month, offline-meet up content, activity/challenge day may also appear. In addition, a major event will have a significant impact upon the calendar. Regular calendar events may be set aside to focus on building up excitement for the event and covering the event once it is in process.

Measuring content

So what do you need to measure? Whether content is successful and which types of content are most successful.

Key metrics

- Number of return website visitors to each item of content.
- Average time spent on each item of content.
- Number of times the content has been shared on other social media platforms.
- Familiarity with other members from the sense of community measurement.
- Average number of visits per member to the community within the past 30 days.

You want to discover which types of content gain the most visitors, the most time spent on the page (the article is fully read), the number of times it's shared externally (word of mouth), and whether members feel stronger levels of familiarity with other members.

CHAPTER 4

Moderation

In the past, the entire role of community management was comprised of moderation. Moderation was defined as removing the "bad stuff." The moderator (usually the webmaster who created the site) would kick out the spammers, remove the off-topic posts, and resolve disputes.

Today we know that moderation is about far more than removing the bad stuff. Sure, it's important that your community is not overwhelmed with inappropriate material. But this is just one part of moderation. Moderation is better defined as facilitation. I especially like how Collins and Berge (1996) classify facilitation. They include the tasks:

1. **Pedagogical (intellectual task): to contribute unique expertise or insight within the content.** As a community manager, you have access to the company, a deeper understanding of the community, and/or experience within the topic.

2. **Social (friendly environment): to promote human relationships.** Also, to affirm and recognize input, provide opportunities to develop a sense of community, maintain the group as a unit and help members work together.

3. **Managerial (organizational, procedural, administrative): set the agenda for the community and overlook the managerial tasks, including managing the flow and direction of the discussion without participants.** Use meta-comments (comments about the discussions themselves) to remedy problems in context, norms, agenda, clarify, irrelevance and information overload.

4. **Technical: ensures participants are comfortable with the technology being used with the ultimate goal to make the technology transparent.**

BARRIERS TO PARTICIPATION

For an organization-based community, moderation is an essential role. Without a moderator, the community may be attacked by spammers, be overwhelmed by conflict, be dominated by a small insider group, be legally liable for actions, burn out from activity, or overload members with information.

Spammers

Unmoderated communities are likely to fall victim to spammers, individuals or 'bots' (software scripts that automatically create many accounts on a website). Spammers post promotional messages to the annoyance of community members.

Spammers frequently overrun unmoderated communities. Spammers drown out the voice of genuine participants and sabotage any meaningful conversation. In recent years registration technology, such as asking registrants an obvious question a pre-programmed bot cannot answer (e.g. *What is Michael Jackson's surname?*), or including a code verification graphic bots cannot read, has helped prevent attacks from spammers.

However, few anti-spam processes can prevent real human beings from registering and spamming the community, and they can be highly efficient. Spammers often only need one response among millions to earn a profit.

Even the most sophisticated technology has not entirely been able to prevent spammers (bots or human) from entering a community and posting promotional messages. Therefore, a community moderator needs to be very aware of this problem and remove such messages quickly when they do appear.

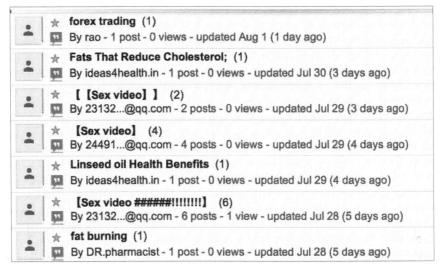

It doesn't take long for a community to be overrun with spammers.

Inappropriate material

The community might be infested with members who repeatedly post inappropriate material that isn't removed.

This material may include *flaming* comments (deliberately provocative attacks on individuals), publishing of off-topic messages to the wrong discussion boards, posting of pornography or illegal software, or thinly veiled messages from members promoting their own businesses.

Information overload

Information overload is an increasingly important concept both in the halls of academia and among street-smart practitioners. A community that becomes too difficult to follow will repel both new and existing members.

Jones et al. (2008) found empirical evidence that information overload constrained interaction. Most notably, they found that 40 participants in an online conversation within 20 minutes was the maximum number that could be sustained.

Jones also found that as the volume of messages increases, users are:

1. More likely to respond to simpler messages.
2. More likely to end active participation.
3. More likely to generate simpler responses as the overloading of mass interaction grows.

A community moderator can help prevent information overload by dissipating activity more broadly into specific interest matters in the community or implementing a tighter moderation policy.

In communities that attract a large amount of activity, such as those listed on big-boards.com, a new discussion can appear and be pushed down off the screen within a matter of minutes. It becomes difficult for anyone to follow a discussion.

Lack of narrative

An unmoderated community lacks a narrative that members can follow. Similar to information overload, it becomes difficult to follow the discussions and individuals no longer feel they are experiencing the community in a similar way. For example, it may become difficult for members to know who and what is popular within a community at any given time.

A community moderator must help create that narrative within the community and provide structure to the daily discussions and debates.

Declining activity

A community moderator plays a major role in stimulating and sustaining discussions within a community. A community without a moderator can struggle to sustain a critical mass of activity. Members are reluctant to participate in communities that do not appear active, yet activity cannot increase without their contributions. A dip in activity can become a downward spiral without a moderator to take corrective action.

ENCOURAGING PARTICIPATION

In addition to removing the obstacles I've described, you also need to encourage members to participate.

This means directly or indirectly stimulating and sustaining activity within the community. This can be done directly (initiating discussions, soliciting opinions to questions, messaging members to invite them to start a discussion) or through more psychological processes (highlighting specific activity, concentrating discussions, shaping motivational community guidelines, etc.).

Moderation activities that encourage participation include:

1. **Guiding members' contributions.** You can do this through both a welcome guide outlining what members should do in the community and a constitution defining acceptable rules of behavior.

2. **Ensuring social density (the amount of activity within a given area) is consistently high without being too high.** You need to dissipate activity when it becomes overwhelming in one area (by creating new areas for discussion, etc.) or concentrate activity when areas of the community become too sparse (removing/combining areas/topics).

3. **Stimulating, initiating, and sustaining discussions.** Proactively stimulating and responding to discussions also involves soliciting opinions from members and highlighting discussions you want members to participate in.

4. **Steering the direction of the community by giving prominence to discussions deserving of more attention.** This involves locking/unlocking threads, creating sticky threads, tweaking the dates or times threads are posted, and so forth.

Key metrics

- Total number of posts per month.
- Total number of active members (refer to active members from the growth section) per month.
- Total number of new discussions per month.

It is not possible to measure the quality of discussions or the steering of the community by any method that isn't entirely subjective. Therefore, I recommend that an independent person is responsible for assessing quality. If you include it as evidence, clear examples should be used that demonstrate where the quality has or hasn't improved.

CONFLICTS AND ANTAGONISTIC MEMBERS

Resolving conflicts and calming antagonistic members can be a time-consuming process. Many community moderators spend the majority of their time resolving disputes between members and complaints against members.

However, few community moderators excel at resolving conflicts, notably conflicts between groups, and many hesitate in removing members.

Community moderators therefore need a clear process to resolve conflicts and handle antagonistic members.

The benefits of conflicts

Conflict in a community does not necessarily hurt the community. Many conflicts between members help develop the community, highlight issues people are passionate about, and increase the sense of community between members.

Scott Peck (1990) identified four stages of community:

1. **Pseudo-community.** This is the first phase where members are keen to get along. Members are usually extremely polite and want to establish a pleasant social order.

2. **Chaos.** Conflict begins taking place between members. Members feel comfortable enough to assert themselves.

3. **Emptiness.** The community lacks a social order after a large number of fights.

4. **True community.** Members have established strong relationships and express themselves honestly and genuinely. Members have developed a process for handling conflicts.

Conflict is an essential stage of community progression. Almost all literature relating to stages of group development refers to a period of conflict in which members express themselves and establish a sense of order based upon an enhanced understanding of each other.

Debates are engaging. Members are likely to participate more frequently if they are involved in a heated debate. Contrary to popular belief that members will leave the community as a result of disputes, there is no evidence to support this theory.

Members are far more likely to leave because the community is boring, i.e. there is little to emotionally engage them. This is common in communities in which there is no friction between members or heavy-handed moderation of such conflicts. For example, if members are engaged in a heated debate about the greatest footballer of all time, a moderator should not lock the thread from further discussions.

When should the community moderator be involved?

A conflict only requires resolution when it becomes an obstacle to participation. Members may be assertive and direct in expressing their view on the topic, but personal attacks cross the line. *"You're wrong!"* is perfectly fine. *"You're a retard if you believe that"* provokes a personal argument, which has no place in the community and offers no benefit to the community.

Moderation is also necessary when the conflict spreads into other areas of the community or overwhelms other discussions. If the same conflict keeps arising, unprompted in a variety of threads, topics, groups or categories, the community manager must step in and resolve the issue between members.

Causes of conflicts

Several competing theories for causes of interpersonal conflict exist but one of the more popular separates the causes of conflicts into five distinct categories.

1. **Individual characteristics.** Conflicts caused by character traits that are prone to antagonizing the other person. For example, an extremely laid back person working on a project with someone with a high attention to detail.

2. **Team characteristics.** Attributes of one team versus the attributes of another. This occurs when the online communities attract segments that may conflict such as those with strong beliefs for and against religion, political groups, or methods of organizing activities.

3. **Project characteristics.** Projects with a tight deadline or that force individuals to work in a manner they are unaccustomed to are likely to provoke a conflict.

4. **Organizational characteristics.** When the organization has overlapping areas of responsibility and competition between individuals for senior positions, conflicts may arise.

5. **Environmental characteristics.** In environments with shortages of resources, adverse conditions, etc., conflicts are common.

Loss of status

Most causes of online conflicts are very similar. Members are concerned about losing status before other members. Because all discussions in a community are public, a disagreement can quickly provoke a defensive reaction that begins a downward conflict spiral. Members feel the need to protect their status in the community.

Two members enter into a perceived zero sum game: for one to maintain status, the other has to lose. However, neither will ever feel defeated and online members will continue debating permanently.

Selecting a strategy to resolve the conflict

Five simple strategies for addressing conflict are:

- **Compromise.** Reach an agreement that meets the needs of both parties—difficult, but the ideal resolution.

- **Accommodation.** Persuading one party to accept the other's demands. You can persuade one member to take the high road or exchange the need to have the last word with a mention in an upcoming news post (or other form of recognition).

- **Avoidance.** Persuading one or both sides to leave the conflict behind without a defined resolution or distracting or otherwise preoccupying members.

- **Collaboration.** Both sides are persuaded to work together to find a resolution.

- **Competition.** Deliberately rejecting the view of one participant to satisfy the other might be appropriate in a conflict between a newcomer and a regular.

Resolving a conflict

Once a member has sparked a conflict that turns personal (or dominates discussions outside of the topic), the community manager should intervene to achieve a resolution.

The community manager must determine which conflict resolution technique to use. Not all of these strategies are created equal. Accommodation and compromise are the most common, with collaboration and competition the least common conflict resolution strategies. Avoidance may serve as only a temporary solution if there are simmering tensions that are not resolved.

To resolve a conflict, you need to interact with all members concerned by e-mail or personal message (not by public discussion). Explain that the conflict is harming the community and it needs to end. Use an e-mail with a cc to all concerned and see if they can chat between themselves and resolve the issue.

You may then create an e-mail outlining the issue and suggesting options the participants may agree on. Each can then reply with their own concerns until they have found a resolution.

Rig the game against the participants

You might suspend both members from participating in the community until they have resolved the conflict. This uses basic game theory to rig the game against the two participants. Members who cannot participate in a community until they have resolved differences have a force compelling them to resolve their conflict.

Escalation against antagonistic members

Many community managers are either too slow or too fast to remove antagonistic members. They either remove the antagonistic member without fully realizing the role this individual plays within the community, or they spend copious amounts of time trying to convert the antagonist into a happy member.

But antagonistic members aren't always bad. They can provoke discussions, highlight topics that other members were hesitant to address, put forward opposing (if unpopular) viewpoints, and prevent *groupthink* in communities. Communities where everyone agrees and gets along are dull.

Even the most antagonistic members can unite the community against them. This sounds crazy (and I've received plenty of criticism for it), but a community united against a few individuals can actually derive benefits.

The question you need to ask is *Does this antagonistic member kill or boost discussions?*

Antagonistic members might not be breaking any rules, but may still have to go simply by virtue of squelching every discussion they participate in. Otherwise, antagonistic members should be allowed to stay because they have a beneficial impact upon the community.

Don't fall into the reactivity trap. Don't get sucked in to spending hours of your time trying to deal with antagonistic members. Make quick decisions and take quick actions.

I often offer clients a six-step escalation process:

1. **Do nothing.** This is my favorite step. It doesn't require much work. If neither the number of participating members nor the quantity of contributions is declining, let it slide.

2. **Reason/befriend/distract.** If the antagonistic member is clearly a problem, you react in one of three ways. First, if it's likely they don't realize they're antagonizing members (this is surprisingly common, usually a personality issue), explain they need to tone their language down because members have been complaining. If they have a genuine grievance or concern, try to ask them what the real problem is and how you can help solve it. Finally, if they are focused upon one particular issue, distract them by giving them a column, or responsibility for a certain topic to express their viewpoint.

3. **Suspend.** If none of the above works, suspend the member and explain why. Suspension can range from three days (one day isn't enough) to one week.

4. **Ban.** If after a suspension they still cause problems, remove them from the community. Lock the account or ban the IP address from registering an account.

5. **Edit/repel.** Some members continue to register new accounts (or mask their IP address). They're intent on causing trouble. Some community managers get caught in a cat-and-mouse game. They ban the new accounts and others continue to spring up. An endurance game, it continues until one side gets tired. It's best left to volunteers. I've had some success by editing comments posted by the member to something softer (usually complimenting other members).

6. **Contact ISP/police.** If the member continues to return or is engaged in threatening/illegal activity, either contact their ISP or the police. You can jump straight to this stage if necessary.

CONCENTRATING AND DISSIPATING ACTIVITY

Your community needs to appear highly active without over-whelming members. This requires the moderator to maintain a careful community-balancing act of concentrating and dissipating activity.

This role is further complicated by the irritation members will feel if the website changes too frequently. Members prefer familiarity in their surroundings. A community that changes its structure too frequently will confuse and irritate members.

The challenge is to balance activity without changing the structure more frequently than necessary.

The activity principle

Another aspect of the moderation role is to sustain consistent levels of social density through the community platform. If one region becomes too popular, it becomes difficult for new-comers and regulars to follow. Over time, a smaller number of members account for increasingly large number of posts.

In this situation, you need to break the community into distinct groups based upon strong common interests. You can use the demographics, habits, or psychographic data to iden-tify clusters of members within the platform who might like a smaller group or forum category within the platform dedicated to that topic.

If any smaller forums grow large enough, it might even make sense to develop a community platform solely for this audience. The Rock And Roll Tribe recently launched a new community Pop Geek Heaven for those interested in pop. It was clearly popular within the existing community so they created a place for it. CoinTalk recently launched StampExchange, a community for those interested in stamps.

StampExchange

Concentrating activity

Many online communities fall victim to having activity spread thinly across too many categories or groups. This causes several problems. First, the community platform feels empty, which dissuades potential contributors from making a post in the belief fewer people will read and respond to their contribution.

Senior Drivers	0	0	No Posts
Teen Drivers	0	0	No Posts
Long Haul	0	0	No Posts
Commuters and Carpools	0	0	No Posts
Safe Driving	0	0	No Posts
Travel and Services	0	0	No Posts
Racing	0	0	No Posts
Offroad Forums: News & Stuff	1	2	Off-Road Vehicles Become More "E... 09-27-2009, 8:05 PM EST By: jackventures
Aftermarket Customizing Forums: Free-for-All , Upcoming Events , Do-It-Yourselfers , Gear Talk , "If I Were You ... " Tips and Advice , Best and Worst Businesses to Go To , Items for Sale , Groups and Clubs	5	7	Should I Upgrade or Stay With Ol... 09-22-2009, 12:09 AM EST By: jackventures
Roads and Traffic	0	0	No Posts

DigMyDrive

This sense of sparseness will also impact the sense of community that members feel with one another. A thin community will appear less successful and members will be less inclined to assume the community's group identity. Members of a genuine community are participating as a contribution to the group's future success. Activity begets further activity, inactivity begets further inactivity.

Also, members will be confused about where to post. The more options there are, the more difficult it is for members to understand where they should post a category. The member has to make a tougher decision. In an advanced community, this is less of a problem. In a community with a low level of activity, it can severely reduce the number of posts.

Finally, posts are less likely to receive a response. Members would have to spend a greater amount of time browsing through mostly inactive categories to find the posts to respond to. This decreases the likelihood of members bumping into each other in their digital discussions.

Slow expansion

At the launch of the community, the number of areas in which posts can be made should be restricted to a mere few, perhaps just one. Only after the community has expanded and information overload is a likely issue should the community moderator dissipate this activity.

An excellent example is the East Dulwich case study. At the launch of the community, there were relatively few categories for members to participate in. As the community grew, so did the number of categories to accommodate what members in the community were doing.

The East Dulwich Forum
The Bishop, The EDT, Inside 72, The Gowlett, The Drum or The Lord Palmerston?

You are here:

Search • Log In • Register

The East Dulwich Forum   T

General issues / gossip
Anything to do with life in London's East Dulwich. Talk about local restaurants, pubs, shops, services, transport, planning, it's up to you...
                                                                                    RSS

Wanted, offered and recommendations
Looking for recommendations about local plumbers, carpenters, cleaners,

The East Dulwich Forum at launch.

This was the East Dulwich community at its launch. The number of categories is heavily restricted to focus activity within key areas.

As the community grew, so did the number of activities within the community.

The East Dulwich Forum

Coffee tastes best at... Blue Mountain? Caffe Nero? The East Dulwich Cafe?

You are here:

Search • Log In • Register

The East Dulwich Forum   Th

⊚ **General ED issues / gossip...**
Discuss life in London's East Dulwich. Talk about local restaurants, pubs, shops, services, transport, planning, it's up to you »
RSS

⊚ **For Sale & Items Offered in ED...**
Sell and give away your articles locally (except family items, see below) »   1
RSS

⊚ **Items wanted in East Dulwich...**
If you want items locally ask for them here.
RSS

⊚ **ED businesses, restaurants & trades...**
Ask for recommendations, feedback and discuss East Dulwich businesses and services.
RSS

⊚ **Residential property in East Dulwich......**
Looking to buy, sell or rent in the SE22 area? Post your property's details or your requirements for free in this section (No agents please) »
RSS

⊚ **The Family Room classifieds...**

The East Dulwich Forum after growth.

Remove and reduce quiet or inactive areas

You should remove or combine quiet areas of the community, where possible, into related groups. If there are barely active groups for members from Romania, Lithuania, Russia and Czech Republic in the community, you could combine them into a more active Eastern Europe group.

But what if Poland is a very active group? Should it also be combined into the Eastern Europe group?

The answer is no. Do not infringe upon a highly active group (or category). It may be perceived as an attack on their group identity. Members are free to join the Eastern Europe group if they like, but it's a decision they can make without interference. The majority will prefer to retain their own group identity.

FireArms created sub-communities for every state in the USA regardless of popularity. States with a high number of members such as Texas are listed alphabetically below states such as Rhode Island, Maine, and Hawaii.

South Dakota Gun Forum South Dakota Gun Forum - Forums for South Dakota gun and firearm enthusiasts to plan shooting events get togethers and discuss Firearms and 2nd Amendment topics related to South Dakota.	**Looking to get into shooting** by maso157 07-06-2012 06:48 PM	2	24
Tennessee Gun Forum Tennessee Gun Forum - Forums for Tennessee gun and firearm enthusiasts to plan shooting events get togethers and discuss Firearms and 2nd Amendment topics related to Tennessee.	**Coming to Gatlinburg** by rsfrid 05-18-2012 10:08 PM	7	36
Texas Gun Forum Texas Gun Forum - Forums for Texas gun and firearm enthusiasts to plan shooting events get togethers and discuss Firearms and 2nd Amendment topics related to Texas.	**Outdoor range - Austin** by jin370 07-26-2012 04:25 AM	44	271
Utah Gun Forum Utah Gun Forum - Forums for Utah gun and firearm enthusiasts to plan shooting events get togethers and discuss Firearms and 2nd Amendment topics related to Utah.	**suggestion on where to move?** by Cat1870 07-23-2012 01:00 AM	7	77
Vermont Gun Forum Vermont Gun Forum - Forums for Vermont gun and firearm enthusiasts to plan shooting events get togethers and discuss Firearms and 2nd Amendment topics related to Vermont.	**The Green Mountain State** by shadow38 07-23-2012 11:07 PM	1	12
Virginia Gun Forum Virginia Gun Forum - Forums for Virginia gun and firearm enthusiasts to plan shooting events get togethers and discuss Firearms and 2nd Amendment topics related to Virginia.	**Gun show at dulles expo** by cvia 07-29-2012 12:22 PM	16	80
Washington Gun Forum Washington Gun Forum - Forums for Washington gun and firearm enthusiasts to plan shooting events get togethers and discuss Firearms and 2nd Amendment topics related to Washington.	**Where are the WA members?** by JustinM 07-29-2012 05:18 AM	5	59
West Virginia Gun Forum West Virginia Gun Forum - Forums for West Virginia gun and firearm enthusiasts to plan shooting events get togethers and discuss Firearms and 2nd Amendment topics related to West Virginia.	**7.65 x 54 argentine ammo for...** by reddawg2001 07-17-2012 09:42 PM	4	33
Wisconsin Gun Forum Wisconsin Gun Forum - Forums for Wisconsin gun and firearm	**Where in Wisconsin you from?** by MiguelAngel	2	51

FireArmsTalk

It would be prudent for FireArms to create sub-communities when there is a clear demand for such a category. Other states could be included in a Northeast category. Meanwhile, Texas itself may need further sub-categories due to its sheer size.

Few communities embrace this approach, however, because they fear it appears disorganized. This is to their detriment. The quest for neat, parallel categories is at odds with the natural evolution of group identity. Do not be inclined to neatly categorize members at the expense of their own group identities. Let these group identities flourish in whatever form makes most sense.

Identifying friendship groups

Another approach to develop a community is to identify friendship groups that are forming within the community and create places for them to talk. These may be open or private. Give them a unique, relevant name. The most successful communities are filled with forums and groups named "The London Shoreditch gang," "The 3am insomniacs club," or "Mike and Joe's freeze-flower forum" not "General Chat," "Advice," or "Classifieds."

These names may make little sense to outsiders but create a strong sense of community among insiders. If you understand the name, it's because you're a member of the community. This increases the sense of identity and bonds between members. Members are more likely to feel ownership over an area of the community.

By embracing a bottom up approach to dissipation, the community manager can be sure that areas of the site will be popular with members and maintain a consistent level of social density throughout the community.

Identify popular topics

Create a new category for popular topics within the community. Identify topics either through their popularity, the frequency with which they are discussed, or their relevance to community members.

The community moderator should carefully watch which topics within a community gain the biggest response. For example, if a frequent stream of people ask novice questions about the topic, the community moderator could create a separate place within the community where newcomers can feel comfortable asking questions and members can go to answer them.

Another example might be the controversial issues you identified in the audience analysis. These issues are likely to consume a lot of discussion within a general thread, so the community moderator might create a unique category for each of these issues.

Identify experts and influencers

A final method of dissipating activity is to identify experts and influencers within the community and create sections that they can run. These people have the authority to bring others with them. They can set the agenda for discussions, moderate discussions and enjoy the responsibility that comes with having direct control over an area of the community.

Experts and influencers can be identified either via the quality of their contributions, the quantity of their contributions or the response to their contributions from others. If the community platform uses online reputation systems, influencers can be quickly identified.

Once a new category/group has been created, the moderator should promote it via the daily news story and an e-mail to members of the community to participate. You should, where possible, also transfer existing discussions on the topic to this forum category.

New groups take a bit of time to get going. Take care to ensure the community reaches the critical mass stage of the community development process prior to developing new groups.

Initiating and sustaining discussions

In the early stages of community development, you will need to initiate most of the discussions yourself. You therefore need to initiate discussions that will engage your members.

There are three types of discussions:

1. **Convey information.** People interact to exchange information with one another. This is the rarest of the three interactions and often misidentified as the most valuable by organizations aiming to develop a community.

2. **Bond with others.** This refers to all conversations that lack purpose, but increase the sense of kinship between members, like chitchat between friends that leads to greater familiarity. When two individuals meet they will commonly interact through safe topics and try to identify a common interest. Through such bonding discussions, members will increasingly disclose information about themselves and gradually trust, and be trusted, by other community members.

3. **Status-jockeying.** Similar to bonding, people interact to defend or increase their status. This is common among existing members, and isn't necessarily bad; having an established pecking order is good for community structure.

The challenge is to initiate the right balance of discussions. A good adjusted balance would be one-third bonding, one-third conveying information, and one-third status.

✉ **Lost coin in the mail** Started by Harryj, 10-30-2008 01:07 AM 1 2 3	Replies: 41 Views: 2,070	Blaubart 07-31-2012, 01:38 PM
✉ **2012 Canadian SD War of 1812, about design.** Started by Whitebeard, 07-31-2012 01:25 PM	Replies: 0 Views: 92	Whitebeard 07-31-2012, 01:25 PM
✉ **Birds from Around the world** Started by arelch, 06-30-2012 09:24 PM 1 2 3 4 5 ... 6	Replies: 87 Views: 988	mrbrklyn 07-31-2012, 01:17 PM
✉ **What's different between contact marks and hairlines?** Started by Aslpride, 07-28-2012 01:13 PM 1 2 3	Replies: 32 Views: 556	TheNickelGuy 07-31-2012, 12:13 PM
✉ **How to grade a proof coin?** Started by Aslpride, 07-31-2012 12:46 AM	Replies: 7 Views: 114	TheNickelGuy 07-31-2012, 12:05 PM
✉ **Building your library on a budget** Started by camlov2, 07-16-2012 05:53 PM 1 2	Replies: 29 Views: 474	medoraman 07-31-2012, 10:25 AM
✉ **Any Numismatic Goals for 2012?** Started by Bart9349, 12-26-2011 06:41 PM 1 2	Replies: 28 Views: 831	medoraman 07-31-2012, 10:07 AM
✉ **Numismatic Malpractice** Started by mrbrklyn, 07-31-2012 03:53 AM	Replies: 0 Views: 133	mrbrklyn 07-31-2012, 03:53 AM
✉ **Great Hobo Nickel Resource** Started by mrbrklyn, 07-31-2012 03:48 AM	Replies: 0 Views: 70	mrbrklyn 07-31-2012, 03:48 AM
✉ **I like Cleaned Coins and you should to thread** Started by mrbrklyn, 04-29-2012 12:06 AM 1 2 3 4 5 ... 43	Replies: 641 Views: 11,734	mrbrklyn 07-31-2012, 03:44 AM

CoinTalk discussions

Intervention

By measuring what types of discussions generate the most posts, you can subtly shift the balance in that favor. This might mean initiating more discussions in that category or bumping/post-dating conversations in the more popular types of discussions.

However, be careful to pay attention to the overall number of responses to all discussions. If you shift the balance too far, the overall number of discussions may fall. While, say, status-jockeying discussions might be the most popular type, if all discussions were status-jockeying, the community itself would become tiresome and participation would fall.

You need to track the overall number of discussions to ensure that this doesn't decline while adjusting the balance of discussions.

Initiating discussions

You can now also use this data to initiate discussions that are likely to appeal to members. Identify which members are really passionate, then ask members to give their opinions or share their own experiences on the topic. You can even ask hypothetical questions.

Examples of possible bonding/status discussions

Common popular discussions in online communities include:

1. **What is your favorite _____? Ask members to list their favorite experiences, objects, or people concerning the community's topic.** It's open-ended and allows for every individual to participate.

2. **What is your average day like? People love to talk about themselves.** We also like to compare our lives to the lives of others. A question along these lines will usually provoke a number of responses.

3. **What do you think about _____? People are keen to express their views on relevant issues; however, they are less likely to ask for the opinions of others.** The community manager can initiate a discussion that asks members to express their opinion on a topical issue and summarize responses they receive.

4. **What advice would you give to someone who _____? Asking for advice is a popular approach to increasing participation.** People like to share what they know. This is a status-jockeying discussion. It also provides a useful vault of information for members to explore.

5. **Can anyone recommend _____? Like the advice discussion above, this encourages status-jockeying as members compete to provide their best recommendations.**

6. **What is the worst thing that has ever happened to you while _____? Discussions that ask members to recount a memorable personal experience are excellent for bonding.** By sharing this information, members are more

likely to like each other. These discussions are also interesting for others to read.

7. **Can anyone fix _____? Present a difficult problem and ask members to submit their solutions.** This is a status-jockeying discussion in which members try to solve the challenge better than others for increased status in the community.

8. **What is the best/worst _____? This is another common post calling for people's opinions on a topic and may be a sub-category within the community's overall scheme.** Questions may refer to equipment, experiences, companies, or products.

9. **Who do you most admire _____? These popular discussions invite members to identify the individuals within the community's sector whom they most admire.** This is useful not only for increasing participation within a community but also for identifying individuals to interview in the community and gathering interview questions.

10. **Is (x) really better than (y)? Identify a controversial issue and use it to spark discussion in the community.** This should be a discussion members will have a split opinion on. It can later be summarized into a content topic within the community.

11. **If you weren't _____would you _____? Create a hypothetical situation and ask members how they would react to the situation.**

12. **Who/What are your top five _____? Ranking is addictive.** Ask members to rank their top five anything. This may lead to an overall ranking for that subject within the community.

13. **How would you handle (topical issue)? If your members were in charge, how would they handle a topical issue in your sector?**

14. **What _____do you use? This discussion is relevant in almost all online communities.** People can compare the benefits of the products/services/equipment that they use. This can also be included as a profile question.

15. Does anyone know how to_____? Does anyone know provokes interest, and the how to can be broad or specific. People are likely to participate.

16. Has anyone tried _____? Again, this is a broad question letting the community moderator stimulate a discussion on the topic of their choosing. Both a bonding and status-jockeying discussion.

17. Is _____right about _____? Take someone's stance on a topical issue and throw it open to comment by the entire community. This can prove an excellent channel to engage journalists within a community and solicit opinions from members that can be used to create a statement/response from the community.

18. Is it ever ok to _____ Another type of hypothetical question, asking members about ethics will stimulate a high level of debate and self-disclosure.

19. What should every newcomer know about _____? This is a fantastic thread for newcomers within the community. It allows members to provide feedback directly to newcomers looking for quality information. These discussions are ideal to be made into permanent sticky threads.

20. **Share your pictures/top tips here.** Sharing advice and pictures can be an easy win for stimulating activity. Try it. I suspect you will find it easy to gain lots of valuable insights.

Your mileage with these prompts will vary. The key is to build discussions around topics that you know members are very passionate about.

Guidelines

It is also possible to optimize the guidelines for the community. However, it's first important to realize that only a tiny number of members read your current guidelines. They have little influence upon member behavior. No amount of tweaking the content of the guidelines will change the behavior of members.

Worse still, the members who read the guidelines are those least likely to break them. Yet members need to know how to behave in the community beyond that which can be gleaned through the social proof provided by other members.

First, you need to measure the number of infractions committed by members during a week. This provides the benchmark against any further changes. Then you need to develop interventions to reduce this figure.

- **Tackle the most common infractions.** One possible intervention is to identify which rules are broken most frequently. You can then either amend this rule (is it preventing members from doing something they genuinely want to do?) or you can publicize it. Send an e-mail or post a sticky thread highlighting this rule and enforcing a one-week suspension for people that break the rule.

  This approach works best when the same rules are being repeatedly broken (perhaps unwittingly), by a large number of members. The goal is to publicize the rule.

- **Tackle the most frequent rule-breakers.** Another approach is to identify those breaking the rules most frequently and directly approach them. This may involve introducing a three-strikes rule, asking the members to stop breaking the rules or having a *wall of shame* for members who constantly infringe against the rules.

  This approach works when it's a relatively small number of members breaking a large number of rules. It means you need to measure the number of rules broken and the number of rule breakers over a one-month period.

Community constitution

Another possible intervention is to give greater meaning to the rules and create a document that is more likely to be read by newcomers and regulars. An online community constitution is a collection of principles established by the community defining the community's purpose and basic conduct.

A constitution should not be established by the organization at the initial launch of the community but should be a process the community is engaged in shortly after critical mass of activity has been achieved.

The community manager contacts founding members and volunteers for their thoughts on the constitution. Together, these few members draft a set of principles for the community. This should be a short document that defines the following:

- **Purpose of the community.** Why does the community exist? What benefit does it provide to members? Is the purpose to exchange information? Give each other a support group? Share emotions/feelings? Make friends with likeminded people?

- **Personality of the community.** Is the community loving? Jovial? Serious? Intelligent? Sarcastic? Let the community members identify the personality of the community. The moderator should be willing to solicit other opinions.

- **Beliefs of the community.** Does the community believe that information should be free? That certain products should be banned? That humor is the best medicine? How could the industry be better? What are the core, sacred, beliefs of the community?

- **Community governance.** How is the community run? What rights/powers/protections do members have? How do members gain more power? What can the community manager do or not do? It is important to define the role of the community manager in enforcing administrative powers.

Developing this constitution is a collaborative exercise. The community moderator must engage members and proactively seek their input (if not entrusting the entire process to volunteers). The purpose is to provide members with an opportunity to develop a greater sense of ownership over the community.

This constitution should be a document that is revised at biannual periods during the lifetime of the community. This allows newcomers to contribute to the constitution and encourages members to again visit the platform.

Once this draft set of principles has been created, it should be presented to the entire community. Input should be proactively solicited in this stage. The greater number of members who participate in this process, the greater number of people will support the community and feel they have a sense of ownership over the very essence of the community. This will lead to increased participation and evangelism for the platform.

Groups are more likely to obey rules they have established than those imposed upon them by authorities.

Welcome guide

A final approach is a welcome guide, a document that subtly guides new member behavior. The objective is to create something positive, not negative.

The welcome guide is a document that explains the culture of the community and helps members to get started. It should be specific in what members *can* do, but it should not appear, nor read, as a *rules* document.

The welcome guide should include:

- **How to get started.** Cover what is new and popular in the community that week. List specific activities members can participate in immediately. Be specific about what members might like to say and how they like to say it (i.e. avoid making errors of etiquette).

- **Community culture.** Detail the culture of the community. Mention any inside community jokes, basic etiquette, rituals and a list of the most common topics. It is also prudent to advise members of what not to do when they make a contribution. What tone of voice, words, topics and language should they avoid using?

- **Community history.** Include a summary of the community's history (linked to after the summary) explaining the evolution of the community. This should read as an interesting guide to the biggest conversation, key moments and controversial issues.

It is vital to measure the success of each of these efforts. You want to see the number of infractions decline and thus free up more of your time for other activities.

STEERING COMMUNITY TOPICS/FOCUS

The community moderator performs a key role of steering the direction of the community. The moderator has the power to spotlight discussions that s/he believes should have greater prominence over other discussions.

This can be achieved through several processes:

- **Bumping.** Bumping a post is a common expression prevalent in forum-based communities. It means to reinitiate activity in a discussion that has dropped down the list of topics, by adding a comment to the discussion, often with the word 'bump' in the post. For example "I'm bumping this post back up, I don't think we quite agreed on this yet." Any member is able to do this.

- **Locking.** In most communities, the moderator has the power to lock discussions. This can be used to prevent discussions from spiralling into personal conflicts, to end discussion on an issue that is causing difficulty to the community or redirect the community's attention to other matters.

- **Unlocking.** The community moderator has the power to unlock previously popular posts for new discussions by new members. This can redirect the community's attention back to popular discussions, stimulate activity, and focus the topical issues within the community.

- **Sticky threads.** Perhaps the most visible element of moderation, the community moderator has the power to give certain threads greater prominence. These might be threads on a topic in which the moderator would like to encourage discussion, attract new members, or reignite discussion on certain topics. Through the simple act of making a thread 'sticky' at the top of the forum page, the community moderator wields a great deal of power and influence over the community.

- **Deletion.** The community moderator may remove inappropriate posts. This should be used as a last resort. It is far more preferable for the member to edit or remove the post themselves.

- **Moving.** A moderator can move discussions from one section of the community to another. This gives the moderator the power to create new forum categories. It can establish a particular focus on a niche topic or redirect many active members to their own place to prevent them from crowding out newcomers.

- **Soliciting contributions from other members.** The community moderator also has the power to solicit contributions from other members to particular discussions. This raises the prominence of some discussions over others. It engages members in some discussions at the expense of others.

These powers provide the moderator with the ability to subtly steer the direction of the community. If the moderator would like a specific topic to be discussed in greater depth, the moderator can find these discussions and give them greater attention. This is a simple nudge to members to participate in these areas.

The moderator should not tell people what to talk about, nor ask them to talk about certain topics. The moderator just gives greater prominence to certain topics and people.

OVERALL GOALS OF MODERATION
Moderation should have goals beyond merely preventing the community from self-imploding. These goals should include one or more of the following:

- **Increase the overall number of participating members.** This is useful for both communities that are growing and those that have a significant participation inequality (a tiny number of members providing a majority of the posts).

- **Increase the number of posts.** More activity from existing members can be measured by the total number of posts to a community within a given time frame.

- **Increase the number of discussions members initiate, leading to greater levels of participation, sense of ownership and activity overall.** The goal is not necessarily to get members responding to discussions, but to get more members to start discussions.

- **Improve the quality of discussion.** Although highly subjective, it's an excellent objective when it fits with the community's positioning and sense of identity. Increasing or focusing the quality of discussions can attract more members and engage them at a deeper level. This will involve steering the community and tighter moderation policies; it's very common in communities of practice and profession. The rapidly growing StackExchange network is built entirely upon the quality of discussions as a positioning tool.

- **Facilitate closer bonds between members to increase the overall strength of the community.**

- **Focus/steer the community toward specific topics, goals, or people.**

Key metrics

Like other aspects of community management, you can use data to measure and optimize your moderation goals. Here's what you need to know:

1. **Number of participating members to show how successful moderation activities are in encouraging members to participate in the community.**

2. **Total number of posts per month for the broad activity success metric.**

3. **Average number of posts per member.** Are members participating more or less than last month? You may want to remove the top and bottom 5%.

4. **Total number of discussions initiated per month.** When combined with total posts, this reveals the average number of responses per discussion per month.

5. **Number of conflicts per month.** Record the number of conflicts you get involved in, and who else participated.

6. **Number of antagonistic members.** Track how many antagonistic members you had to deal with and at what stage in the escalation process you stepped in.

Don't make casual inferences. As *Black Swan* author Nicholas Taleb is fond of pointing out, with so much data available to us, it's easy to find things that correlate. If you look hard enough you might find the growth of your community closely matches the average rainfall in Venezuela...which doesn't mean you need to make it rain in Venezuela to grow your community. Be careful about what you're measuring in the community and its connection to the actions you take.

## CHAPTER 5

Influence and Relationships

Imagine that you wanted your members to do something very specific in the community tomorrow. Perhaps give you feedback, welcome newcomers, talk about a particular topic, or help organize a certain event.

How would you achieve that? The truth is your powers of persuasion are restricted to one of three categories:

1. **Content creation.** You can send news content or e-mails to the community en masse. You can highlight trends or opportunities within the community and shine the spotlight on members whose actions merit reward.

2. **Administrative rights.** You have the power to remove people and posts that are not suited to the website. You may also grant rights and access to members of the community. You can change the structure of the site to highlight areas you want members to participate in.

3. **Access to the company.** You have the ability to gain exclusive news and outcomes from the organization. You are the link to the company. You can convey their view, and perhaps even get some free products for community members!

You can tell members to do what you want, but that doesn't work so well. Members hate being told what to do. Worse still, members might feel they're being used. Your control over the community is clearly limited. If you want your community members to do certain beneficial things, you have a challenge. How can you influence the community?

HOW A COMMUNITY MANAGER CAN WIELD INFLUENCE

The two best ways to influence the community are:

1. **Become an influential member of the community.** Be highly active, gain credibility, and be well-liked by members. You literally become an influential member of the community. People respect you, trust your opinions and are happy to do what you say.

2. **Build relationships with influential members of the community.** The second approach is to then work *with* these members to make things happen within the community. This is a consultation process in which you actively seek out their feedback and build a base of support for what you wish to achieve.

Let's tackle becoming an influential community member first. In 2007, Robert Cialdini published a terrific book outlining six paths to influence:

- **Reciprocity.** If you do something for someone, they're more likely to do something for you.
- **Consistency.** People act in ways that are consistent with what you have said and done previously.
- **Liking.** If people like you, they're more likely to do what you want.
- **Authority.** If people see you as an authority figure, they're more likely to do what you say.
- **Social proof.** People do what they see other people doing.
- **Scarcity.** People don't like losing the opportunity to get something.

You can use several of these paths as methods to influence the community.

Gaining personal influence in the community

How you participate in the community will determine whether you are able to influence the community. In many communities, the community manager acts as an aloof god-like figure using the three powers (content, administration, access) to cajole people.

At best, this approach limits what you can achieve in the community and at worse alienates your community members. You may become perceived as a negative authority figure within the community who prevents members from doing what they want.

This can lead to resentment and deliberate attempts to sabotage what you're trying to achieve. Believe me, it's very hard to do your job when your community doesn't like you. Not only will members not do what you ask, but they might proactively do the opposite.

Therefore, if you wish to gain personal influence in a community, you need to participate in a manner that will gain you influence. The following three paths are the most effective means to become influential:

Likability

A powerful magnet, likability is a clear and measurable strategy to gain influence in the community.

Likability requires two consistent attributes: positivity and friendliness. Positive people are significantly better liked than negative people. Positivity is reflected in the tone, language, and actions you adopt. Try to be consistently optimistic, use positive language, speak about opportunities arising in the community and inject positive emotional language into discussions.

Friendliness means you need to interact with a large number of individuals in the community. Your mantra is to be friendly and frequent. Be highly active in the community and engage in dozens of conversations on a daily basis.

Friendliness involves having a sincere interest in other members of the community. Dale Carnegie, in his classic 1936 text *How to Win Friends And Influence People*, identifies several elements for befriending others. These include:

1. **Show genuine interest in other people.** Ask members about their lives, how they're getting on, what's new.

2. **Talk in terms of the other person's interest.** Talk about topics that members are interested in (not just you). Refer specifically to their own interests or experiences.

3. **Make the other person feel important, and do it sincerely.** Highlight how the member is helping you or others in the community. Make them feel good about themselves. Make members feel their contributions are worthwhile.

4. **Show respect for people's opinions.** Regardless of your own beliefs, show interest in someone's opinion and give credit to their belief.

5. **Admit mistakes.** If you're wrong, admit it quickly. Members respect you more for it.

6. **Appeal to noble motives.** Talk in terms of greater goals. What is the member trying to achieve in the community. What is the goal of the community? How do the two align?

7. **Show praise.** Frequently praise the contributions of members—achievements or things they are planning to achieve.

8. **Don't criticize or complain.** Relationships can turn negative quickly. Don't let that happen to you.

These time-tested techniques are relevant for building relationships both inside and outside of communities.

If your approach to building influence within the community is likability, you need to be *consistently likable*. You don't get to have off days. But likability is not suited to all community managers. It's mentally exhausting, takes a lot of work, and simply doesn't fit the personality of some community managers (not all community managers have an excessively upbeat, outgoing, personality!).

Reciprocity

Another path to gaining influence is reciprocity, the social law that one action will be met with a similar action. If you punch someone, there is a great chance they will punch you back. If you buy them a gift, they will probably buy you a gift. Better still, if you help them move, they might cook you a meal later on. Positive reciprocity builds trust between members. Negative reciprocity begins a downward spiral.

However, reciprocity is not necessarily even. Gifts may not be of equal value. The quantity and quality of exchanges may increase or decease over time. In addition, there need not be a specific count of gifts sent and received. Indeed, the idea of a gift itself is misleading. A gift here refers to actions that beget similar actions (compliments, advice, etc.).

You may increase your influence within a community by initiating a reciprocity cycle with members. This is a long-term strategy through which you try to help members with any problems (related to the community or not) with a view to building up a reciprocal influence.

Proactively interact with members, find out what problems/challenges they have (or might have), and identify ways you can help them. This is more about an increasing number of small gestures as opposed to letting members use your beach house for the weekend.

Expertise

The final popular path to gaining influence is to provide remarkable value and expertise in every interaction. The objective is to be perceived as a highly regarded authority on the topic in the same vein as some academics. The mantra to this approach is *interact less, but better*.

In *every contribution* you add unique insight or value that cannot be gained from elsewhere—exclusive information, a deeper analysis of the situation, or a new perspective.

You spend less time interacting with individual members and more time making sure your contributions are respected and help you become an authority within the community. Although not the easiest approach, it's my personal favorite. It is suited to community managers who might find the previous two approaches difficult to sustain.

Befriending influential members

The second route to building influence within the community is to build relationships with top members. You should invest time in building relationships with your most influential members. These members give you influence over the community. Many community managers complain about being unable to make the community do what they want but don't invest the time to build relationships with their key members.

Having a high level of influence is important if you want to extract value from a community. For example, if you want members to give you feedback on a product or service, asking them too generally yields disappointing results.

Members hate being told what to do. It's better to use social proof, to show them people who are already taking that action. If a member sees 20 people talking about the pros and cons of particular product features, they're far more likely to join in.

THE KEY RULE OF COMMUNITY BEHAVIOR IS

The biggest influence upon a member's behavior is the behavior of other members.

In any situation, people generally do what they see others doing. Some supporting studies are as illuminating as they are horrifying. Solomon Asch, or the more entertaining Dan Ariely, found the behavior of individuals, whether giving the wrong answer to an obvious question or cheating and stealing, is heavily influenced by those around them.

This presents a chicken and egg problem. How do you get those first members to start doing what you want so you can influence the rest of the community? The answer is to build strong relationships with your top members.

Optimizing relationship development

Relationship development follows a common pattern. Initially members will meet and begin safe discussions to look for an area of commonality. If they find this common interest, they will discuss it for a period of time.

Over a series of discussions, they will begin to talk about other topics and disclose increasing amounts of information about themselves. A reciprocal process that builds trust between members, this disclosure begins in relatively safe areas, such as likes and dislikes, and steadily progresses to more personal issues.

Step 1) Initial discussions

The first step in the relationship development process is to open that initial dialogue. Online, this can be more difficult than it might appear. There are two reasons for this. First, members can be very busy. Given their work e-mails and social lives, responding to an e-mail from the community manager might not rank highly on their agenda.

Second, you're competing against takers and spammers, against people who ask for things in their first e-mail. If you have a blog, you're almost certainly bombarded by dozens of e-mails a day from people who want you to write about a specific topic, participate in their event/activity, or promote their infographic (please stop this!). Anyone who tries to make you do something in the first solicitation is a *taker*. We're pretty good at identifying these people, regardless of how flattering their approach may be.

You're also competing against the spammers. These are e-mails from people you don't know trying to get you to do everything from sending bank details to collect an inheritance to clicking dubious links. We have a low level of trust towards messages from people we don't know. It's a natural defense mechanism. But it does make life a little more difficult for people trying to build genuine relationships.

You're not going to build a strong relationship based upon a single e-mail, so please don't even try. What you do want to do is establish the basis for a good relationship. Your goal in that initial outreach is to solicit a response.

The initial message is an icebreaker that provokes a response based on standard conversation analysis theory. The opening conversation starter is likely to be one of the following:

- **Asking a question is the most common conversation starter.**
  The question should be relevant to something that the individual has done in the past. This question can then be built into a relationship. If you know the recipient spent a year in a monastery in Tibet, you might want to ask a question about it. If you know they're from a certain location, you might want to ask about that. If you know they are interested in a specific topic, you might want to ask about that.

- **A comment the other will agree with is more common in specific situations.** Passengers may criticize an airline company if they are delayed and seek approval from others. This agreement is a prelude to further discussions.

- **Praise, always a great way to begin a conversation, can be as simple as, "I like your shoes."** Praise for previous actions, praise for positions, experience, or skill often (within reason) forms the basis of a conversation. Praise should be specific and genuine and should relate directly to a member's contribution to the community.

Your data should indicate which approach tends to work best with your target audience. It might be entirely random, but this is unlikely. Using the data about which type of approach works best, you should gradually be able to refine and optimize this approach.

It is important that there is no intention to request the recipient to do anything favorable for you/your community/your organization in the initial contact. All you want to do at this stage is to identify what the recipient has done in the past, and ask a question, state a comment, or give praise based upon that.

Assuming you get a response, the next stage is to repeat the process again. You want to sustain that discussion. Based upon the content of the response, find another question to ask, praise to give, or a comment to make that will further the discussion. This gets easier over time.

Once you have exchanged a few e-mails, you can move to the self-disclosure phase.

Step 2) Self-disclosure

In the self-disclosure phase, you want the recipients to share thoughts, experiences, or details about their own lives with you.

The best way to do this is to share something yourself. If you're having a discussion about golf, you might try to slip into the discussion your first golfing experience, what you hate/like most about golf, or what golf clubs you use.

If your self-disclosure is reciprocated, you can then share a little more. This is a gradual process. It might not begin or end with a single e-mail exchange. It might take place over several months.

Step 3) Shared event/activity

Once you have established a good foundation for a budding friendship, you can move on to a shared event/activity to solidify this relationship.

This shared event/activity doesn't need to be huge. You don't need to go out for beers together (although this would undoubtedly help). You just need a time-limited activity that you both can participate in. Perhaps a phone call to discuss something relevant to the community, or perhaps an upcoming community event, a focus group, or an in-person meet-up.

Again, data will come into play and help you identify what shared event/activity works best.

Step 4) Sustained relationship

Congratulations, you now have a relationship! Yet as your diminishing relationships with your college buddies can attest, friendships need to be maintained or they fade. You therefore need to make a genuine effort to sustain these relationships. This means checking in at least once a month.

Checking in is a time-consuming process, but it keeps the relationships strong. As much as this doesn't sound very friendly, I suggest you schedule it. Have a set time each month that you dedicate to building and sustaining relationships. If, for example, you have four hours a week to spend on relationship development, schedule two hours every Friday and Monday to contact the 50 to 100 people you're trying to sustain relationships with.

You can't remember every detail about every one of these relationships. So either use your e-mail history to refresh yourself, or create a spreadsheet that keeps notes on the development of this relationship—the same way you would for customers in general.

The people you sustain relationships with will change over time depending upon your criteria. If the criteria shifts, you might want to let a few of those previous relationships fade in favor of those who more closely match your criteria.

Interventions

You can break relationship development down into its unique stages for online interactions. Some might object using data to measure something as sacrosanct as relationships. But that data makes you *better* at building relationships.

Key metrics:
- Number of members approached to open initial dialogue
- Number of members who respond to initial discussions
- Number of discussions advanced to self-disclosure
- Number of members who participated in a joint/shared activity with you (the community manager!)
- Number of members with whom you maintain an ongoing relationship (minimum one discussion per month)
- Number of members in the insider group/volunteers

Imagine these stages as a funnel, similar to the newcomer conversion funnel on page 63. From the total number of members you approach to build relationships, not all will reply. From these, not all will participate in a sustained discussion and disclose much about themselves. Of those who do, not all will attend a shared event/activity and from them even fewer will become sustained relationships.

Once you know specifically where the process is faltering, you can identify how best to optimize this process.

Using the data gathered above, you can pinpoint where most relationships are faltering and test different approaches to reverse it. If you're losing them very early, then the initial outreach might be wrong. You might be using the wrong ice-breaker, or the approach might not sound truly genuine.

If you're not getting past self-disclosure, then you need to try a different approach. Maybe you're going into this stage too early, or the information you're sharing about yourself isn't right for building a relationship.

If you're not getting past the event/joint activity stage, then consider this a more relaxed phase. Try a simpler event. Try inviting the recipient to participate in an issue in real time or get their opinion on relevant things in the community. This just has to be a single thing that you're both participating in together. You can mix and match an array of different ideas here.

For a sustained relationship, this is usually a case of balance. You need to maintain contact without having too much contact. Too much contact can seem draining or needy. I personally schedule this, but perhaps you can try other approaches to maintain contact. How about a regular discussion? Or identifying ways you can help that person? Or send that person something of interest to them (like a news clipping/link)?

This is a process-driven approach. You might not get it right the first time. You just need to get it right over time.

The relationship criteria

Once your community surpasses a few dozen members, you can't have relationships with everyone. It's more useful to have several dozen high-quality relationships than a few hundred poor-quality relationships.

Should you build relationships with the members who make the most contributions? Have the most friends? Provide the most expertise? Are most passionate about helping out? It depends on your relationship strategy.

Your criteria for relationships will usually involve one or more of the following:

- **High levels of activity.** The most active members will often be the most influential members. However, this is not necessarily the case. The most highly active members may also be those who most desire influence as opposed to having influence or most prone to engaging in a dispute. So, while the correlation is strong, it is prudent to use high levels of activity in conjunction with other criteria listed here.

- **High levels of expertise or passion for the topic.** A member with a high level of expertise and passion for the topic may be an ideal individual for the community manager to befriend. Their expertise or passion can be identified via their contributions. You can look for exceptional insight or value added across several conversations, emotive use of language when discussing topics, or reference to activities or properties owned when discussing the topic.

- **Distinctive contributions.** Most communities have people who make a unique contribution, from a cartoon series featuring community members, to a poem, video, or special way of making their point. They may be prime members for befriending and engaging in the community at a more committed level.

- **Interesting real-life positions.** When members fill out their profiles, look for individuals with specific attributes. This may include people with a senior job, who live in interesting locations, or who have unusual experience.

- **Emotional intelligence.** Members with a high level of emotional intelligence may be identified by their response to criticism or when they try to resolve disputes rather than antagonize others. If your community is struggling with a large number of puerile disputes, you may look for members with high levels of emotional intelligence to change this culture.

- **Great contacts.** Individuals who have excellent connections to VIPs and influencers within the sector may also be worth engaging in an insider group. Identify them through mentions or relationships on other networks.
- **Strategic fit.** Finally, some people are just a great strategic fit for your community. They have expertise, experience, enthusiasm or opinions in an area you would like your community to move into, possibly a sub-category of the community's overall topic.

EVOLUTION OF RELATIONSHIP STRATEGIES

A community manager can only maintain a limited number of *strong* connections at any given time. Past a set number (usually between 30 to 60) additional relationship activities may be to the detriment of all bonds. You must prioritize relationships based upon the contribution to the community.

The relationships you develop are not static; they evolve over time and shift from sets of individuals to other sets of individuals as their commitment and influence rises and wanes.

You should also reassess the value of these relationships against the cost of maintaining them. This cost includes other members with whom relationships could be developed and the time that could be spent on other activities.

Seeking opinions and the reciprocity cycle

During discussions, look for opportunities to disclose information about yourself. Information may include feelings on relevant topics (*I like/hate ___*), passions, or experiences. If your disclosure is reciprocated (i.e. recipients begin disclosing information about themselves), greater levels of disclosure can be encouraged.

Also look for opportunities to discuss off-topic issues, especially those relating to the individual's everyday life, or hopes, fears, and ambitions. Usually people only share like that when they've developed a degree of trust.

Finally, look for opportunities to initiate the reciprocity cycle. Identify something you can do to help the individual: find information, recommend something specific to them, or give advance notice of a relevant topic.

Building an insider group

Building relationships with key members is essential, but it's better to convert these members into an insider group that interacts not just with the community manager, but also with each other.

An insider group serves several purposes, including:

1. **Rewarding key community members with greater trust, influence, and power.** Members like to be rewarded for the contributions they have made to the community.

2. **Solicits invaluable feedback from members about what the community is/isn't doing well.** You need to know what your members think about the community.

3. **Recruiting platform for volunteers to help manage areas of the community.** The insider group is a go-to place for finding volunteers who can help you manage the community as you grow.

4. **Shows you listen to their opinions.** Members want to know they have the ability to change the community. This increases their sense of ownership, which in turn influences their participation level and advocacy for the community.

5. **Co-creates the community strategy and makes things happen within the community.**

It is the final point, *making things happen* within the community, which is the group's most important function. They create the social proof for other members in the community.

The community manager needs to proactively establish this group from an early stage of the community's lifecycle. Initially, the insider group will be the founders of the community. As the community evolves, the group will expand to include both veterans and newcomers.

Principles for growing insider groups

There are several key principles for growing insider groups in the community.

1. **Headhunt members of insider groups.** The insider group must be representative of the community and not solely those who put themselves forward. Include a broad mix of individuals who have something to contribute to the group.

2. **Heavily moderate discussions and schedule actions.** This group has a specific purpose and requires a tighter level of moderation than other parts of the community. Keep a clearly defined list of tasks that this group should be doing with fixed deadlines, e.g. opinions for change of site design by November 2nd. The group must have clearly established discussion topics and a summary of the group consensus.

3. **Rotate membership.** Rotate members over a period of time depending upon their levels of activity and quality of contributions. It may be appropriate to invite people to a fixed term of participation of three to six months and then renew that term for longer durations.

4. **Build the group early.** The community manager should start this group very early on. Initially comprised of the founding members of the community with newcomers invited based upon their contributions, the group should expand as the community grows.

5. **Publish membership of the group.** The group's existence should be transparent. Its purpose and list of members should be published within the community for members to

see. This gives members recognition but also ensures the non-insiders know that this group is representative of the community. It alleviates potential mistrust when dramatic changes are made within the community and identifies individuals that members may wish to contact.

6. **Name the group.** The insider group should have a name that is a symbol used within the community. This name should not be linked to any association with authority over other members. Such a name will provoke a negative backlash from community members.

7. **Publish the outcomes of the group.** The community manager should publish the summary of what the group has decided. This should include which members made what contributions and how this will affect the community in the future.

Insider groups and volunteers

The insider group and volunteer group overlap but are not interchangeable terms. The insider group provides feedback, advice and actionable support to things that will be happening within the community. The insider group primarily supports the community at a social/interactive level. The insider group provides the community manager with influence over the community.

The volunteer group supports the community itself. The volunteer group works on more functional/technical levels. They create content, moderate areas of the community, invite members, and proactively work to develop the community.

Many members who are involved at the insider level will also be volunteers. However, volunteers require far greater commitment and reliability than insiders. Not all members of the insider group will be able to offer this level of commitment, but should not be excluded due to limited time commitments.

VOLUNTEERS

As the community grows, you will no longer have the time to perform all the key functions. An online community requires volunteers to scale up. In order to recruit volunteers, you need to understand their motivations: the need for efficacy, recognition and financial gain.

Efficacy

Efficacy is the individual's need to have an impact upon their surroundings. A major motivation of a volunteer is to have real power to make a difference within the community.

A volunteer with the power to remove negative members and content might have a heightened sense of superiority. The volunteer may also want the power to create content or change an area of the site. Sometimes the volunteer may simply like having a direct influence over the direction of the community and act at a higher, strategic level.

Power, alone, is not traditionally the strongest motivator for participants of the community. It is usually a precursor to a stronger motivator, recognition.

Recognition

Recognition is the strongest motivator among almost all contributions to a community. Recognition is the sense of joy achieved when a contribution receives attention. This confirms to members that they stand out.

Volunteers are not commonly the community's most influential members. Influential members already have a high level of recognition among the group. Volunteers are usually mid-level community members who want to be afforded the attention of the community but lack the ability of the top community members to achieve such status.

Financial gain

In many communities, volunteers participate in the hope of some later financial gain. This may be in search of a job position as a community moderator or an indirect opportunity.

Crafting a community role

Use these motivations in crafting a role for volunteers in the community. A common mistake is to assign a volunteer to the work the community manager doesn't enjoy: work that is repetitive, redundant to the success of the community, or given very little exposure.

Few volunteers will stay for long in such a diminutive role. The need for recognition and power will drive the volunteer to seek better opportunities. Offer the volunteer prominence and power with work that is critical to the success of the community and is highly visible to members.

Of course, a volunteer's role must derive from an essential need. For example, if the forums of a community platform are continually overrun, you may decide a volunteer could help. The volunteer role should not simply be to remove bad content from the forums. Instead, it should be a broader role that covers both support in removing bad content from forums but also offers a variety of more interesting work.

Work might include creating content for the community, submitting opinion pieces, finding VIPs to interview, helping arrange events, or taking responsibility for certain forums. These roles combine the less exciting work of a volunteer with work that is more highly stimulating.

A role may also be built on what a member is already doing within the community. For example, if a member frequently highlights bad material that has been posted within the platform, the community manager may formalize the role to include real powers to resolve such issues.

Creating a volunteer role

A typical volunteer position has the following elements:

1. **A name.** *"Community volunteer"* is a poor choice of name that, for many members, may possess negative connotations (cheap labor!). The role should have a name that engenders a sense of pride and power within the community. This may include any variation of *community function* and *admin-related* terms. For example "Content Chief" or "Jujitsu Trend Hunter" or "Community Name Champion."

2. **Functional roles.** Include the specific functions that need to be performed. For example, keeping check on the forums analyzing data, welcoming new members.

3. **Power roles.** Include the ways volunteers will have a degree of power within the community. This might be administrative privileges and the ability to add, remove or change areas of the website.

4. **Recognition.** Include ways members receive visibility in the community. This might be creating signed content, or gratitude for arranging significant events.

Recruiting volunteers

There are two approaches to recruiting volunteers for the community, headhunting and soliciting applications.

Headhunting volunteers

Few members will volunteer for anything that sounds like unpaid work. One way around that is to position the role as valuable and sought-after by headhunting specific members.

Identify people who have already made a significant contribution to the community and offer the member an opportunity to be more involved. This volunteer position can then be announced on the website, which in turn may make other members more receptive to recruitment overtures.

Converting an active member into a volunteer may be a steady process in which voluntary roles begin with minor contributions and gradually grow into more extensive responsibilities. For example, if a member writes a lengthy and informed answer to a discussion topic, the community manager may invite her to create a weekly column on the post. If this is successful, she may later be given responsibility for a forum category based upon that topic, possibly being in overall charge.

This can eventually be made into a formal volunteer role. Should this member ever leave, it can be a role that is advertised to the community and someone else can fill the spot.

Community members with enthusiasm for one area or interest within the community are likely to also become interested in the community as a whole. If the community manager encourages the slow development of this involvement, they may eventually become valued volunteers.

Soliciting applications

Good volunteers are invaluable to a community and they should not be recruited en masse. Each volunteer should require and receive personal attention. This will provide them with both the increasing motivation to become a volunteer and the knowledge to do their role effectively.

It is essential to recruit volunteers as individuals and to gradually work on getting these individuals more involved in the community. This may involve recruiting volunteers in single file and ensuring one is successful and happy in their community role before trying to move on to another member.

Volunteers should not be taken for granted. They will need constantly increasing opportunities and influence over the community.

Recruiting alternatives

An alternative approach to recruiting volunteers is to call for people to support this community. You can periodically create volunteer opportunities, and then write a news release asking members to put themselves forward for the role. A number of individuals who would be willing to support the community beyond the initial specified role may emerge.

The community manager may also have a continually updated *get more involved* page on the community platform that would detail the process of becoming a volunteer. List the current volunteer vacancies within the community and invite members to apply for those in which they have an interest.

Ask for specific help

If you can persuade someone to volunteer to help out any element of your community once, you are highly likely to be able to convert them into committed volunteers for the community.

Ask members to support a specific activity that is taking place within the community or ask for specific help on a relevant issue. For example, you may call for advice from members on a particular area of web code and then work with those who give advice to become regular volunteers.

Alternatively, you may host an event or webinar and ask for volunteers to help support the event in some fashion. Each person who steps up can potentially be converted into a regular volunteer.

Measuring and developing relationships

Several key metrics can gauge your success in building relationships. The first is the number of developed relationships you've sustained with key members. This will indicate whether the relationship building process has been a success or whether there are flaws.

If the number of sustained relationships is low, analyze the process, message by message, to determine where the response ends. This may be, for example, between the second and third e-mails (assuming you're using e-mail), when the conversation fails to progress beyond the initial question.

It is very easy for the community manager to build successful relationships with members who have little influence over the community; it's more difficult to build relationships with members who can succeed in influencing the community.

The only way to measure this is to assess how many community activities achieved a critical mass of participating members. If the insider group/relationship group is not being positively used, then the time spent on this activity is wasted.

Measuring relationship development

Now you want to measure how successful your activities have been. This includes measuring:

1. The number of successful activities initiated by the insider group.
2. The number of active members in the insider group.

If members in the insider group haven't made a contribution within the past month, you should remove them.

CHAPTER 6

Events and Activities

Events play an essential role in the growth and development of communities. They unite audiences and create the social foundations for great things to happen.

Events can make communities more fun and provide constant activity. Events give members a reason to visit frequently to see what is happening in the community and provide motivation for lurkers to participate. Events can also provide a structure for the community. Members know what to expect and when to visit.

Chalip (2006) is a keen proponent of using events to support a community. He writes, " . . .*event organisers and host community planners should foster social interaction and prompt a feeling of celebration by enabling sociability among event visitors, creating event-related social events, facilitating informal social opportunities, producing ancillary events, and theming widely.*

The resulting narratives, symbols, meanings, and affect can then be leveraged to address social issues, build networks, and empower community action."

Sense of community experts McMillan and Chavis (1986) claim events are a key component in increasing the *shared emotional connection* between members. Events are a social lubricant that facilitates a strong sense of community among members.

Young et al. (2011) go further in describing benefits of events. They believe events help bond and increase participation in a community. They also note that events give communities a sense of history and purpose. Events encourage individuals to directly interact with each other. Such interactions are vital in facilitating trust and relationships.

The benefits of events, however, are not limited to offline communities. Several studies have shown that events have a strong beneficial impact upon online communities.

IMPACT OF EVENTS UPON ONLINE COMMUNITIES

Young et al. studied the impact of offline events upon online communities and discovered offline events can increase page views by 60.4% and participation by 27.2%. Likewise Cluett and Seah (2011) noted that interactions and conversations between fans are "*most vigorous during times of major events.*"

Events provide the context for many positive contributions to a community. Some of these are as follows:

- **Events provide increased contact between individuals.** The contact hypothesis (Allport, 1954) states that contact alone increased liking between individuals. Simply by having an excuse to connect with each other, the strength of relationships and bonds increase. This improves activity over the long term.

- **Events celebrate the community identity.** Community members feel a sense of pride and an increased sense of community (often known as *communitas*).

- **Events initiate leverage to sustain broader community goals.** After the 1992 Barcelona Olympics, the partnership and sense of collaboration and togetherness was used to regenerate a vast area of the city.

- **Events breed a shared sense of history.** McMillan and Chavis (1986) noted the remarkable connection between a shared sense of history and community events.

- **Events can help recruit volunteers to the community.** Once people put themselves forward, they identify with the volunteer model. Event volunteers can be converted into regular helpers and supporters of the community.

In addition, there are economical justifications for events. Organizations can use events as a source of revenue for either a) supporting the community or b) increasing company profits.

Organizations can earn income with entry fees, by selling items during the event, or through finding additional event sponsors. In some online communities, such as World of Warcraft, comic books or alternative lifestyles, events have become major international festivals in their own right.

Elements of successful events

Fredline et al. (2006) list different elements of successful events.

1. **Anticipation.** The community must anticipate the event. Many organizations drip-release information about activities/performers/speakers over a period of time.

2. **Reason to participate.** A strong theme/performance/draw makes more people want to attend.

3. **Opportunity to interact with others.** The event should not be solely about the performance itself.

4. **Clear sense of closure.** A summary and roundup can be effective.

5. **Engagement with the host community.** It's essential that participants engage with the host community both before and after the event. Events should not be forced upon a community.

Different types of events

Events can be categorized by venue (online/offline), frequency, size and purpose.

Most online communities only host online events, but this may be a mistake. Offline events have a far greater impact than online events. A single offline event can achieve more than dozens of online events. Such events solidify existing relationships members have with each other and provide the platform for a rapid growth in activity within the community.

The frequency of events determines whether the event is a regular and expected interaction designed to breed consistency, trust and entertainment between members, or whether the event is a one-time ceremony and an opportunity to celebrate or commemorate something of significance.

Events range from those held regularly, such as a weekly or monthly live discussion on a topic, to those only held to commemorate special occasions, such as a product-launch or milestone achievement within the community.

The size of the event usually is based on the number of members involved. Size varies considerably with few agreed upon metrics. In some communities, the weekly discussion or interview is attended by far more members than any irregular event. In other communities, the size is inversely correlated with the frequency. The longer the time between events, the more people attend.

Finally, events can be categorized by their stated purpose. Some events are intended to inform and educate members. These include conferences and exhibitions. Other events are for pure entertainment. These include social gatherings ('*meet-ups*') without any formal activity.

General meetups cannot be held on a large scale; there needs to be a common focus and structure for the social elements. Many people need an excuse to interact. That's why most social events are designed around an activity e.g. drinking, bowling, playing cards.

Regular online events

Frequent online events are a staple of successful communities. Accessible to all members, and held at specific times, these events increase the sense of social presence (the feeling that you're interacting with an '*intelligent other*').

You should schedule online events on a weekly and monthly basis. Events may include:

1. **Webinars.** An interactive presentation in which the community manager, a member of the community or an expert on the community's topic delivers a presentation online and answers questions from community members in real time. A variety of software (GoToMeeting and WebEx) can host such events.

2. **Themed discussion.** Each week, you can set up a live chatroom for your members to participate on a predetermined topic. Issues may be rotational with different members guiding the discussion from week to week. On Twitter, for example, #cmgrchat is a weekly discussion for community managers.

3. **Weekly interview with a VIP in the community's sector.** People of power, fame, expertise and those with unique personalities, this list may include managing directors at relevant companies, skilled experts (such as those designing products or doing something unique within the community), or those who have an interesting personality. You can use a moderated live-chat or solicit questions from members in advance.

4. **Competitions/challenges.** A regular competition can be a quiz, or a skill-based challenge. Some communities, for example, ask members to submit their favorite community-related stories or photos and nominate a winner each week. It might be possible to find sponsors to support these events with free products/vouchers for the winners.

5. **Newcomer orientation.** Once a month, a community may host a day to welcome new arrivals in the community. Regular members can introduce themselves, set up some basics threads for newcomers, and help teach members about the culture of the community.

6. **Promotional days are a way to provide access to sponsors and opportunities for community members.** Promotional days might include price discounts on products/services, promotions from one member to another (by dedicating a day for this, self-promotion on other days might be alleviated).

All these regular events can be held at frequent intervals. Different events will be suited to different audiences. Some will be looking for traditional entertainment, others will be looking for information and tips leading to self-improvement within their topic.

Regular events also encourage frequent activity within a community and build expectations from members for regular interactions. This frequent activity builds a consistency of interactions between members that leads to trust, a key component of successful relationships within communities.

Irregular online events

Communities should also host irregular events not held at fixed intervals. These events celebrate a community's achievements, bring audiences together for a specific purpose, or promote the community to external audiences.

1. **Milestones.** The community should celebrate significant milestones—the community's 10-year anniversary, the 10,000th active member, 50,000 posts in a single month or achievements such as causing significant change in the community ecosystem.

2. **Fundraising days.** A community may host a fundraising day or week for a set cause. Fundraising has many benefits; it's a clear investment in the community's success. It creates a common goal that increases a sense of achievement or failure, which can significantly improve the community (even a failure can help bring a group together!).

3. **Broader victories and celebrations.** A community may celebrate something relevant in the ecosystem such as the

success of a VIP, a legal ruling in the community's favor, or the end of a negative trend.

4. **Product launches.** A community might celebrate the launch of a new product or service by building anticipation, including a gossip column about possible features of the product/service, introducing a live-blog leading up to the launch, or initiating threads asking members to submit their views and thoughts. These threads will be sticky for the day or week.

5. **Member achievements.** Celebrate achievements like the release of a book authored by the member, a birth of a child, a wedding, the launch of a new company, or anything else the member takes pride in.

6. **Hall of fame induction.** Some communities have introduced a hall of fame for individuals within their ecosystem. Have your members done something great recently? Induct them into your community's hall of fame.

Irregular events should be considered special and uncommon. There should be no more than one irregular event every two months. This ensures that irregular events are rare enough to generate excitement and intrigue within the community.

Regular offline events

Offline events may be a great means of promoting the community to a broader audience and recruiting volunteers who will also support the community's online activities.

Most importantly, offline events solidify online relationships. Contacts, which may initially be formed online, are cemented through real person interaction. In addition, in-person contact can spur new relationships and a greater sense of community among members.

I was 14 when I attended my first offline event for a video gaming community that I had been actively participating in for two years. Many of the relationships I made there, I still have today—13 years later.

Types of offline events

A community may organize many types of offline events, from exhibitions or conferences held in large entertainment venues to weekly meetups in local bars, cafes and libraries.

In practice, most offline community events are regular, held on an annual, bi-annual or quarterly basis. However, smaller events and gatherings do play a role in both larger communities and those localized around a specific area.

Communities that are either localized around a specific area or have clusters of members living in close proximity may consider holding a regular meetup. Usually a monthly event, members gather in a nearby venue (usually rented) and talk about their community's interest. This requires very little planning and, indeed, might be organized by community members.

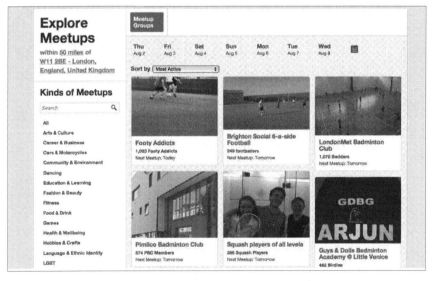

Meetup.com

Frequent events are common among groups organized using Meetup.com. Meetup organizers usually book or borrow a room in a pub/bar, café, office or community hall at minimal cost.

More successful meetups (50+ attendees) may recruit sponsors to pay for the costs of the event.

Decentralized gatherings

Some communities with a large following have recently begun asking members to organize their own local events. Mashable selects a day and then invites members to create events for people to attend near their city.

Mashable Meetup

Mashable sets a day and invites people around the world to

use meetup.com to establish their own events, which are promoted through the site.

Larger events are likely to be held annually or quarterly. Mid-sized events may be held bi-monthly or monthly. Smaller events can be held weekly. With the exception of communities based around a common location, it is rare for a community to host weekly offline events.

Ensuring events are held at a consistent frequency helps to create proper expectations, anticipation and, most importantly, the sense of closure between the end of a previous event and the beginning of a new event. Sense of closure to events is essential to improving the emotional connection among community members.

Events a community may organize include:

1. **Exhibitions for the community's topic.** This might involve inviting relevant organizations to showcase their products.
2. **Product launches.** A community can actively participate in a product launch for a product/service they are excited about. This should include entertainment, free samples to review, and competitions/challenges.
3. **Conferences.** A community can invite the most prominent individuals in its sector to speak about the topic. Talks might be expertise advice, personal stories, or information about current trends or new ideas.
4. **Trade shows.** In many sectors, a community may organize a trade show to explain market trends, talk to other members about their activities, and spotlight new ideas in their field.
5. **Themed parties.** A large themed party related to the community's topic for members, who can dress up and just have fun, is a win-win.
6. **Entertainment shows.** The community may host a show for members. For example, a community about skiing could showcase movies of skiing videos, letting members submit their best clips.

7. **Unconference.** Recently, *unconferences* have grown in popularity. At an unconference, any attendee is allowed to post a topic to discuss and stake out a spot within a venue for those interested to gather around and listen. This informality provides a casual and innovative environment for ideas and close bonds to develop.

Large events are usually based around a clear informational, educational, or entertainment benefit with a multitude of smaller informal events. For example, most major business conferences are based around a series of formal talks from respected individuals. However, they also include a variety of parties and networking events for attendees to meet and interact with each other.

It is important that large events allow as much time for individuals to speak informally in small groups as they do listen to any central speaker. In most modern events, the time allocated to networking or socializing exceeds the time spent on the main attraction.

Planning

Large events take considerable planning to execute properly. A badly organized and executed event will generate resentment from attendees. The organization should allow six to 12 months for planning, promoting, selling tickets, and making bookings/arrangements.

I also highly recommend hiring an experienced event planner for a large event. Event organizers understand the complexities (and regulations) of hosting events that the organization may not.

Imitate existing large events

Most organizations benefit from copying an already successful event. By imitating an event in a similar field, the organization can mitigate many of the risks involved in hosting a large-scale event. Copy negotiating discounts at nearby hotels, using similar sound and seating arrangements, selling tickets at a similar price and imitating similar topics of discussion.

The community manager should be developing content for the event (previews, reviews, announcements), promoting the event externally to potential member groups, and soliciting volunteers to help plan and run the event.

Content before the event

The purpose of content before the event is to build anticipation for the event itself. For smaller, regular, events, this will likely be a single post. For larger events, it might be a series of posts over several months. Content includes:

- **Initial announcement.** Release some basic details about the event and when registration/sign-ups will go live.

- **Drip information.** Release a steady stream of announcements about the event at frequent intervals. Announcements may include the speakers/entertainers for the event, confirmed new activities at the event, and a special offer for attendees.

- **Pre-registration announcement.** For a first-come, first-served event, stating the registration will go live in (x) number of days can encourage people to purchase tickets sooner. For the first few to register, you could include a special offer such as a discount or free product sample.

- **Registration announcement.** The announcement that registration is now live should include all of the previous information as well as a clear call to action.

- **Number of registrations/speed of registrations.** Many events later publish the number who have registered within a short time or the speed of registrations if the number is not apparently high, e.g. 100 people purchased tickets within the first hour as opposed to 150 have purchased tickets in the first week.

- **Interviews with key individuals about the event.** The community manager may interview speakers or participants in the upcoming event and include questions from community members.

- **Event previews.** The community manager may preview the event, outlining the highlights, asking members what they are most looking forward to, and creating an air of expectancy. What are people wondering will happen at the event? What mystery exists about the event?

- **Registration closing.** The community manager should announce when event registration ends. This may even include a countdown. Alternatively you could post how many tickets remain with frequent updates as this number declines.

- **Final details.** A day or two before the event, post practical information about getting to the event, emergency contact details, and any other logistics.

During events

Publish frequent content during the event. You want to make members who didn't attend feel regret over not having attended, but also stay informed so they are not discouraged from participating in the community after the event.

This content could include:

- **Live blog.** Similar to the blogs adopted by many news organizations during major breaking stories, a community could have a frequently updated live blog as the event progresses.

- **Interviews.** Interview members from the community during the event to give live reactions and publish this on the community website.

- **Photos taken by community members and by the community manager can be published and frequently updated during the event.**

- **Video footage.** Short video clips showcasing what's happening at the event can be published during the event.
- **Daily summaries.** The community manager should post round-ups after each day of the event summarizing the major activities and any surprising news.

After the event

Events need clear closure to sustain the sense of community among members and cement the event into the community's shared history. Closure may require more than one post on the event.

- **Conclusion and thank you posts.** Following the event, write a summary and thank members for attending. This should be informative and provide individuals who couldn't attend a clear overview of the event.
- **Highlights/top 10 features.** Post the event highlights as voted by members, possibly with other rated elements such as the 'person of the event' or 'newcomer' mentions. Any in-jokes may also be mentioned.
- **Call for suggestions for the next event.** The community manager should also publish a post requesting suggestions for the next event and constructive criticism of the recent event.

Measuring events

You want to measure whether the events you organize are successful. To do this you measure both the overall goals of events and then each particular type of event.

The overall goals of events are:

1. **Increase activity.** Events should produce significant bumps of activity, followed by a prolonged, above-average increase.
2. **Sense of community.** You need to track members who you previously surveyed to see if their sense of community has

increased since participating in events (and compare this to members who didn't participate in events).

3. **Increase number of participating members.** The number of members that participate in the community should increase as a result of this event. The newcomer to regular conversion process might also reveal this.

4. **Growth/attention spikes.** You can also track any growth/attention spikes related to the events. Did events bring in a flood of newcomers to the community? Did the event cause a spike in attention outside of the community during that time? Compare the date of the event (and those a day or two either side), with growth in the community.

Since introducing events, has the level of activity, sense of community and number of participating members increased? These figures will show if events are successful.

Now you need to determine how to improve events. This process is very similar to optimizing content within a community. You want to identify which types of events are most popular.

To optimize events you need to benchmark and test the following:

1. **Which types of events gain the highest levels of participation?** Obviously you can't compare regular online events with irregular one-time events. Compare the same type of regular, online, events with one another to identify which get the highest levels of participation. Remember, you're looking for categories of events, not individual events.

2. **What event times are most popular?** You can benchmark what time the event is held with the attendance number. By testing different times you can establish which type of event works best.

3. **What type of promotion for an event achieves highest number of registration/attendances?** How do members hear about the event? The promotion for an event has a significant impact upon whether members attend. Do short posts with a

registration link lead to the highest number of signups/attendance? Do long, explanatory, posts with clear details of how to attend and what to expect work best? Are multiple posts required? Should you have a repeating schedule event where members only need to register once?

Try to change single elements at a time to test what works best. It should take three to six months to test the variables described above and enhance your events.

CHAPTER 7

Business Integration

This chapter is for readers who are building a community for an organization. We will review what an organization needs to provide for an online community to succeed and how to harvest value from the community.

It might seem counter-intuitive, but it's entirely possible for an organization to have a very successful community that yields absolutely no benefit to the organization.

Business integration and strategy are what separates a professional community manager from an amateur. A professional community manager can integrate the business into the community, build internal systems, and ensure the community generates a defensible Return on Investment (ROI).

The community manager should be constantly striving for better business integration. Recently the term *social business* has gained popularity. Whatever you call it, the objective is to ensure that the needs of the business and the community are as closely integrated as possible.

The community manager should:

- **Ensure the community is delivering value to the company.** You need to proactively measure the ROI and establish the value of your community. You need to work towards increasing that value.

- **Ensure employees participate in the community.** If your employees don't participate in the community, why should your customers? When employees participate it increases the perceived value the organization places upon the community. It also ensures you are able to respond to technical questions members might ask.

- **Integrate the community with the four P's: product, price, promotion and place.** You might try to develop community-branded products or ask the community for feedback on products. You could provide special price discounts to members or promote products through the community. You might let customers buy items through the community.

Key metrics
- Number of employees participating in the online community.
- Number of processes (promotion, price, distribution, product) that have been adapted to suit the needs of the community.
- ROI of the community.

OPTIMIZING BUSINESS INTEGRATION

The community can gain influence over the company itself in beneficial or non-beneficial ways. For example, while one upset customer is not a major cause for concern, when many echo one voice, it's a problem.

Customers can now organize themselves against the organization. They can speak negatively online, arrange boycotts, and attempt to change the way the organization conducts itself. Many organizations have cause to rethink a community approach.

Yet the negatives are outweighed by the positives. A community can become an invaluable testing group for product and service development. Members can feel involved and engaged, creating a sense of ownership that makes them promote the company to others.

The integration challenge

Many organizations stumble when they create a community but then fail to respond to members. For example, some companies have developed listening stations to understand and respond to customer complaints or suggestions. Yet few actually change the product or service in response. The company may apologize, send out replacement products/services, but not make the changes required to prevent further complaints.

Feedback and innovation

Many organizations create communities for feedback, research, and innovation opportunities. Communities are a cost-efficient alternative to traditional focus groups and market research firms. They can provide early warning of upcoming problems and ideas for future development.

They can also be a potent source of data mining. By developing a community, organizations collect invaluable data concerning the audience's demographics, habits, and psychographics through sentiment analysis and tracking prompted and unprompted feedback.

Sentiment analysis is the process of reviewing online conversations as to whether they show a positive or negative sentiment towards the organization. Such analysis can reveal how recent announcements, products, or other activities have changed how members feel towards the organization.

By correlating sentiment with activities, the company can see whether it should review or change its products or services.

Unprompted negative feedback occurs when members are concerned enough with a problem that they feel compelled to post about it online. The issue affected members so much they either sought help online or complained about it publicly. This is a significant step (assume most people are lazy!) and their feedback is more valuable.

When the organization seeks specific advice from the community through events, surveys, content, interviews, discussions, or specific online focus-group activities, it's prompted feedback. In prompted feedback, members when pressed may highlight aspects of the product/service that they might not be happy with, but this may have no influence upon their buying behaviour. However, the organization may then invest considerably in *correcting* this apparently large problem.

Alternatively, an organization may have an ongoing *'what can we improve?'* section on the website that allows members to make suggestions. Dell and Starbucks use an idea generation/ranking platform, where members can vote each other's ideas up and down. The most popular ideas rise to the top.

Once a community is launched, the organization must be willing to incorporate feedback into future product/services. Failure to do so might upset their best customers. Positive ideas are best gained from prompted feedback, while unprompted criticism is more important from a future product development perspective.

Packaging

In addition to incorporating feedback, the organization may also develop packages specifically for community members—special branded versions of the product/service. The packaging may reflect unique characteristics of the community or include features that the standard package does not. For example, when promoting *Tribes*, author Seth Godin included pictures of 3,000 community members on the inside cover of the book.

In addition to unique physical packages, community members who purchase the product/service might gain bonuses that non-members are unable to acquire. For example, an opportunity to visit the company HQ, attend a call with the CEO, free invitations to upcoming events of interest, or discounts on other products.

A secondary benefit of this approach is non-members are more likely to join the community to acquire this benefit.

Automation

It may be useful to ensure that members who purchase a product/service are automatically registered for the community. GiffGaff admits a large number of newcomers into the community this way.

GiffGaff

Automation is not always possible, however. It is sometimes easier to include a free invitation to join the community in the packaging/receipt of existing products/services. This is an ideal audience that may significantly contribute to the community.

The ultimate goal of integration is to develop products for the community, not a community for the products. This means using the community to identify the dream product/service and then using the resources of the organization to create it.

EMPLOYEE INTEGRATION

The community manager often is the only link between the organization and its community. The community manager updates the organization about the community and updates the community about the organization.

This is not an optimal process. It increases reliance upon one individual, limits the level of enthusiasm for the community, and restricts the community from directly interacting with those responsible for the products and services they support. It also directly limits the levels of participation and enthusiasm *from* the community.

While helping staff members participate in social media platforms, blogs, social networks, and microblogging networks has been emphasized, little attention has been paid to staff participating directly in an online community—or whether this is a good idea.

The problem with one representative

Such lack of participation has a negative impact upon a community. The community manager often lacks depth of knowledge about a product.

Specific questions about the organization or its products may go unanswered, or take considerable time to answer. This reduces the likelihood of the community becoming an alternative (and superior) customer service channel, and decreases the level of activity in the community.

I believe one aim of the community manager is to increase the number of staff members directly involved in the community. You should seek to influence staff members and encourage them to participate directly in the community.

Increased loyalty

If community members are able to directly interact with the organization's staff, they become more likely to develop positive opinions of the organization. They begin to identify as *one* with the organization, a common aspect of cult organizations identified by Douglas Atkin in *The Culting of The Brand*.

Oneness means to feel the organization represents them, which increases loyalty to the organization and subsequent purchase behavior. You cannot achieve oneness by keeping the community at a distance from the rest of the organization. Staff members must actively participate in the community with clearly defined personalities.

Increase employee participation rates

While many organizations attempt to mandate employee participation in the community, this is rarely a success. The most likely participants in the community are those passionate about participating in the community.

However, there are a number of tactics that can work in engaging an employee in the community. These include:

- **Interview an employee for the community.** Ask for opinions and comments on the interview. I bet your employee joins in the conversation. Then get him/her to interview someone else for the community. People like to feel important.

- **Introduce them to fans of their work.** If they work in marketing, introduce them to people who like their marketing materials.

- **Talk about your employees in the community.** No one can resist learning what people are saying about him or her.

- **Employee of the month.** Every month let the community vote on their favorite staff members from a list. Those with no votes might decide it would help if people knew who they were—and what a way to improve customer service.

- **Give an employee an assignment for a four-week advice column on one specific aspect of your product or service.** They might just enjoy the interactions and fame.

- **Online customer complaints.** Be bold. Build a specific place for online customer complaints. The community can complain about products, specific staff interactions, or anything they like.

- **Encourage direct communication.** Ask the community to send feedback and recommendations directly to the employee's e-mail address.

- **Challenge/competition.** Ask the employees to run a competition, challenge or innovation project related to their field of expertise.

- **Give power and responsibility.** Give employees the power to moderate and be responsible for a forum/group within your community.

- **Bring up the community in every staff meeting.** What are the latest news, developments, ideas and complaints? What are the broad overall trends? What are the clear actionable insights? What are the case studies?

- **Only let the top employees participate.** Once you've reached top employee status, you can join and represent the company to the community. Now everyone wants to participate.

- **Set an employee versus community competition.** What's a big challenge facing your organization? See who comes up with the best solution.

- **Participatory content.** Start a series all your employees can be involved with. How about "Day in the life of ____". It's easy and builds relationships with members.

Above all, look for opportunities involving responsibility, fame, and ego over financial incentives. Being rated and judged by the community is a powerful motivator.

Personalities

The personality of staff members has a significant impact upon whether members develop positive feelings towards them. A common error organizations make is to *restrict* the personality of participating staff members.

Restricting staff members from expressing opinions on topics, participating in off-topic discussions, revealing any personal details about themselves, or using informal language—all such restriction is a mistake. People like to interact with genuine individuals, not faceless, generic company representatives. It is difficult to like someone who is unable to express a personality, talk about interesting topics, or engage in a genuine debate.

Staff training

While it is necessary to train staff members on how to deal with a variety of community situations, the training should be a guide to contributions as opposed to restricting contributions.

- **Training in how to deal with difficult questions.** Questions might include asking the employee's opinion on the stances of organizations, particular products, or broader political/ religious issues.

- **Advise participating staff members to avoid questions likely to provoke a strong reaction.** Preface their opinions with *in my opinion*, and be honest if they aren't able to comment *(e.g. "As an employee, I can't comment on the issue")*.

- **How to deal with difficult members.** Staff needs to use a simple response for dealing with members of the community who try to goad them into a heated debate. I recommend a one-response process before dealing with the matter privately.

- **What not to talk about.** Staff members should be aware of off-limit subjects: legal matters, sensitive information, details of an upcoming product, or any insider news.

- **Personal safety.** Staff members should be aware that community members may attempt to contact them through other social channels, such as Facebook, Twitter, or e-mail, which is rarely a good idea. I suggest staff do not accept or engage in discussions with customers through these channels.

- **What to talk about.** I also recommend preparing staff for topics they can talk about: insider information they can reveal, popular themes in the community, and upcoming events.

- **Crisis communication.** It's rare an organization faces a genuine crisis situation. However, staff should be prepared for a scenario in which 10,000 community members and 300 journalists are hounding them for a response to a major product/service/organization fiasco.

I recommend developing a series of practice scenarios based on each of the situations above for staff to try to navigate.

Track employee participation rates

You need to track how many employees from the organization actively participate in the community and try to increase that number. This can prove difficult as most employees are busy and will resist being *forced* to participate in the community.

By tracking the open rates, you can benchmark existing employee contributions and test different interventions until you identify what works in your community.

Distribution

It might be suitable for some organizations to integrate the distribution of their products/services within the community. This will involve the timeliness of purchases, the accessibility of the purchase, or the place of purchase itself.

Allowing members to purchase the product or service in advance through the community is likely to attract many people to join the community, which in turns yields benefits for the organization. It may also be feasible to accept a limited number of pre-orders through the community to stimulate attention and embrace the scarcity principle.

You might also allow members to purchase the product directly (or exclusively) through the community. Again, this attracts more potential customers to the community that may yield benefits such as decreased marketing costs, greater loyalty, and further advocacy among their existing social circles.

PROMOTION

You should use the community as a vehicle to promote the organization—but without oppressing the community.

It would be bad practice, for example, to continually push new products and services upon the community. Frequent reminders to purchase will cause members to think of the community as a cheap marketing tool.

This can provoke a negative backlash, disillusionment with the community, or the proactive boycott of the organization by community members. The organization can directly lose the money invested in the community by decreased sales from existing members. The organization must use a value exchange whereby members receive value (tangible or intangible) from the promotion itself.

Approaches to using the community as a promotional vehicle include activities that focus on existing members and activities that focus on non-members via referrals and word-of-mouth.

Promotion to existing members

If an organization wishes to excite existing members about upcoming products/services/news, it needs to offer value beyond self-promotion. This might include providing the community with exclusive information before anyone else.

By receiving exclusive information the community may feel better appreciated for its support. Exclusive information can come through many channels:

- **Q&A session with company representatives.** You can schedule regular live events with company representatives. During these events members may ask questions about future products/services and receive a response. You may also host an event where members can ask questions and seek support about a specific upcoming product/service.

- **Drip-release news via the forum.** Members can learn more about the product/service without a formal announcement. This is also likely to attract more people to join the community because they are drawn to the original source of rumors or information. It may also inspire relevant journalists to join the community.

- **Invite members for sneak previews.** An organization can invite its active members for a preview of the product/ service. This might be a first-look opportunity or a hands-on demonstration. This acts as a reward for active members and can encourage positive word-of-mouth. If the organization allows photography, videos, and information sharing via social media platforms, previews can have a significant reach and generate a large amount of interest.

- **Let members test the products/services.** The organization may send top members free samples of products/services (similar to review copies for journalists). This builds anticipation and encourages potential members to participate more to receive a free sample.

Price

Three methods to integrate price with the community are discounts, premiums, and new pricing structures.

Discounts for community members

If community members receive a discount code to purchase a product or service, it increases the likelihood they will purchase the product (all discounts do). This yields relatively little benefit to the organization. It may instead reduce the revenue from the organization's best customers.

However, if the discount is promoted so widely that it encourages non-members to join and participate in the community, this may counter the loss of income from the best customers. As more non-members are converted into regulars, the benefits to the organization continue to increase. If discounts are offered, they should be promoted externally as well as internally.

Discounts for non-members

A widely used method to stimulate referrals is to provide members with a discount code they can share with friends. This must be integrated into the process of joining the community. For example, the shared discount can only be redeemed when the non-member registers for the community through the shared link/code.

Discounts for most active members

Discounts for the most active members (or longest-serving/ regulars/highest reputation score) encourage other members to increase their level of activity in anticipation of future discounts. Increased level of activity improves the community as a whole and should yield benefits over the long-term—higher levels of growth, sustainably higher levels of activity, and an increased sense of community.

New revenue streams

Discounts are only one method of integrating pricing with the community. The danger with discounts is reduced revenue from the organization's best customers. In addition to discounts, you can look for opportunities to use pricing to earn more from the organization's best customers.

One method of increasing revenue for the organization is to charge a membership fee to join the community. This can be a one-time fee or a recurring monthly/annual fee (a combination of both works best).

When a membership fee is charged, you need to provide benefits in addition to a standard forum/social network. This might include user guides, opinion columns, and an array of other opportunities.

A membership fee might be included in the pricing structure for the product itself. This can be especially useful for web-based products, which already offer a variety of pricing structures.

Promoting the community

In addition to promoting the organization to existing members, you should promote the community to non-members: other customers.

Promotion can include securing coverage in relevant trade magazines, mentioning the activities of the community in newsletters, featuring community activities on the organization's main website, or encouraging relevant event attendees to join the community.

By promoting the community, you increase the status of members in the community. Members see their group featured in other channels. As a result, they are more likely to participate and identify with the group's success.

## CHAPTER 8

Return on Investment

Let's begin with a simple proclamation: many organizations develop online communities based upon objectives that aren't suited to communities, for example, to reach new audiences.

It sounds like a reasonable goal, until you consider the following...

Why would someone join and participate in a community for a product they don't buy? Why would people want to spend their spare time talking about a product/service they don't yet purchase?

With one exception I'll explain later, communities work best for existing audiences, those who have already shown an interest in the topic. Communities don't create this interest, they capitalize upon it.

Realistic objectives for developing a community that *can* create an increased ROI include:

1. **Increase loyalty.** Whoa, wait-a-second.... this sounds suspiciously like *engagement*. Loyalty isn't the end goal. Increased retention, repeat purchases... that's the goal. Sneaky loyalty... very sneaky! You see how easy it is to track the wrong things?

Let's try again. Loyalty can be split into different objectives that are more quantifiable such as increased retention of existing customers and increased repeat purchases (get your customers to spend more with you—wonderfully known as *share of wallet*).

1. **Increased retention of your existing customers.** It costs more to acquire a new customer than to keep an existing one.

2. **Increased repeat purchases.** Get customers to spend more money with you. This might be by buying premium-level products/services, using your product/service more frequently

and buying replacements or simply buying more because they like you more.

3. **New revenue opportunities are similar to more money from existing customers.** However, I want to separate it as it might involve identifying sales revenue opportunities that people aren't already familiar with.

4. **Reduce marketing costs.** Spend less on other channels as a result of the community. If, for example, all your target audience were members of your community, would you still need to buy time/space in other channels to reach them?

5. **Feedback/innovation.** Generate new product ideas. I'll explain more on this later as it presents something of an ROI dilemma.

6. **Reduce customer service costs.** If members are increasingly turning to the community to ask questions/get help about the products, this might either increase retention or decrease your customer service costs, which can be measured.

7. **New sales leads.** Using the community to generate new sales leads is very common in business-to-business communities for high-value (expensive) products.

8. **Recruitment.** An online community can be an effective re-cruitment tool, a substitute for headhunters. It can save you time on these tasks and provide you with access to those who are most knowledgeable and enthusiastic about your products.

When you boil down these community objectives, it becomes much easier to measure fairly accurately how successful you are at each one. You just need to collect the data in a clear, defensible manner.

Defensible is the operative word. It's easy to magic up a few ROI numbers. It's harder when you have to defend them. You have to prove that you didn't make the numbers up. Now let's review how to measure each of these ROI goals.

Increased retention and repeat purchases

Compare the beliefs and behaviors of people when they first join the community to after they become active members or split test those whom have purchased similar amounts prior to joining the community.

Take a group of your medium-level buyers. Compare those who join the community with those who don't to see if the former now purchase more.

If you can't measure this exactly, then use sampling across the community. Sample the pre-/post-purchasing habits of 100 members at monthly intervals. Over a period of time, you will gain a fairly good understanding about whether the community impacts how much customers purchase from you.

At this stage, some community managers complain they simply don't have this data. Okay, fine. Sure, you might not have the data, but there is no excuse for not starting to collect this data now and having it within three to six months. Why don't you compare, for example, how much of the product/service members buy as they join the community (use their e-mail address to track their purchases) then measure this against their habits six months to one year later?

You can do a *random controlled trial*. You take a similar group of customers, invite half to join the community and, six months later, compare this half with the half that you didn't invite. What impact did participating in the community make?

Remember, you're not looking at any one individual's habits at this stage; you're looking at the group's habits. Of the, say, 100 people you invited to join the community — how many continued to purchase from you six months later? Of the 100 people you didn't invite, how many stopped purchasing from you?

While it may be tempting to have a graph showing the launch of the community and overlay that with broad retention rates for all customers, this is phenomenally inaccurate. There are a variety of factors that cause the trend to sway one way or another. For example, the time of year can make a huge difference. People buy more of most products in December than they do in July.

If only 3% of customers are active community members, it's dumb to say that the community made any difference to the total customer base. But comparing that 3% of customers who are members against a similar 3% who are non-members is a valid method.

Reduced marketing costs

If you gauge the hypothetical reduced marketing costs without actually reducing your marketing costs, that's not a valid method. Advertising value equivalent is no measure of success.

The problem with reduced marketing costs is connecting it to community activity. A company going through a recession might slash the advertising budget. That doesn't mean the community was responsible for the advertising budget. (There's one of those potentially misleading correlations again…)

What you need to determine is whether the advertising budget was slashed while sustaining the same level of sales among the target audience thanks to the community. Again, you need a customer file to determine this.

Feedback/innovation

This cannot be meaningfully assessed through metrics. If a community generates the idea that becomes a bestselling product, how do you assess the value of that? Do you attribute all sales of that product to the focus group? What about the marketing of the product? Don't they deserve some credit?

It may be possible to use a community instead of focus groups, in which case, the cost of focus groups can be included as a return. Yet this does not account for the value of a good idea.

The marketing/sales effort can make or break a good idea. The same idea might flourish or flounder depending upon whether the advertising campaign was any good. A bad idea with a great marketing effort can generate considerable profit.

And this isn't just limited to the marketing/sales effort. It extends to all aspects of the organization. The best way of determining the value of an idea is to isolate it from all other aspects. This isn't something you can easily do. However, you can include anything extraordinary as a sub-note in your calculation.

Reduce customer service costs

Here are two true statements:

1. It's not a good idea to build a community for customer service.
2. Most successful communities are customer service communities.

Why the contradiction? It's part definition, part logic. First, the definition.

'Online community' is a much-abused term. In current usage, almost any group of people interacting online is being referred to as a community, even if these people don't even know each other (even if they *hate each other!*).

We do a terrible job at distinguishing between different social groups online. In the *real world*, we have mobs, tribes, crowds, audiences, gatherings etc., but online, we just use 'community.'

An online community is a group of people who have developed relationships around a strong common interest. If they don't interact with each other, haven't developed relationships with each other, or don't share a strong common interest, they're not a community.

In most *customer service communities,* people who have a problem with the product visit, ask a question, receive a reply and leave. They don't build relationships with each other. Therefore, by definition, these *are not* communities.

I'm not denigrating these efforts; I'm highlighting that, by definition, they're not communities. They're customer service channels. They can be very effective customer service channels, too. This can be productive and generate a clear ROI for the organization, but they're usually not communities— regardless of how we abuse the term.

So what's the other problem with these channels?

They often miss the point. Imagine you have 10,000 people visiting your customer service website every month. A company might celebrate and highlight how useful the channel is—hurrah!

Can you spot the problem with this thinking?

Having 10,000 people who need help with your product isn't necessarily a good thing. It means you're creating faulty products. It might make sense to invest more money on resolving the issues as opposed to responding to them.

However, in successful branded communities in which members do genuinely build relationships with each other, there is often a support element. People with problems or questions about the product tend to visit and check the community first before calling the customer service line.

How do you measure that? You look at whether the customer service costs have decreased. Has the volume of calls/e-mails gone down? And if it *has* gone down, can you reduce staff costs as a result? If so, you can include this figure in your return. If not, sorry—it doesn't count. You can't use a *cost per call* here if you haven't actually made a real savings by reducing the number of staff required to handle calls.

New sales leads

A friend of mine launched a small, exclusive recruitment community in London. He had been struggling for some time to get his service noted by the key influencers in the area, so he launched the community to bring them together.

He hosted regular events and got to meet all the top executives in the industry. As a result, he was able to speak directly with the executives and learn about their problems. He could make suggestions. Soon he was generating multiple sales opportunities and was closing about 50% of them.

Measuring new sales leads is a relatively easy process. You calculate the profit of the sale. However, as with *feedback/innovation*, taking credit will confuse other factors that helped close the deal. For example, it's hard to close a sale unless you have a good product to sell.

You can include the entire profit derived from that sale within the return figure of the community.

New revenue opportunities

Many possible revenue opportunities may arise from community development. If you host community events, charge fees for attending or find sponsors for events, the profit can be included. If you develop special-edition products for the community, the added value of these should also be included.

There is no shortage of possible merchandise or unique products that can be sold to community members. In my earliest video gaming communities, people used to pay a monthly fee for *'bouncers'* to hold their name in the chat room. The odds of someone wanting your specific name were small, but this didn't stop people paying money to have a small program hold their name while they were away.

Recruitment

There are two sides to returns from recruitment. On one side is the cost savings usually involved in the recruitment process. On the other is the performance of those recruited from community channels.

Online communities can be an excellent source of finding employees. You can develop a community as a recruitment tool and use it to gather the smartest people in your industry. Your community will contain those who are most enthusiastic and knowledgeable about your brand/industry.

Imagine, for example, if you regularly posed questions to your community asking for their expertise. Imagine if you got to know the people that were most helpful, intelligent and had a proven track record of great contributions. You can recruit directly from these people.

Again, there are two benefits—the cost-savings and the potential superiority of recruits found through the community. Let's tackle the cost-savings first. Recruitment can be an expensive process. You might need headhunters or recruitment agencies, and all of those efforts are costly. If you develop a community as an alternative to this, any money you no longer spend on recruitment costs (job advertising, agencies, headhunters, etc.) you can now record as a return.

WHY ALMOST ALL ROI EFFORTS ARE FLAWED

How do you accurately measure the ROI of an online community? Before I tell you how, I want to warn you of the biggest
mistakes commonly made when trying to calculate the ROI of
an online community. These include not measuring the ROI,
trying to use a single, simple, repeatable formula, trying to be
too precise, and using the wrong metrics.

ROI Error 1 — Not actually measuring the return

Non-analysts use metrics that do not directly lead to increased
revenue or decreased costs. This is common in formulas such
as ROE or any measure of *wow, thank you, buzz, klout.* Some
practitioners use metrics of engagement, loyalty, collaboration and sentiment.

These are not financial metrics. They do not show an
increase in profits for the community. A community can significantly increase the level of engagement or loyalty without
increasing the profits of the organization.

Data mining expert Kevin Hillstrom recently shared the
story of an organization that boasted about the success of increasing engagement with customers, while the number of
repeat buyers continued to decline. There is a clear discon-
nect between engagement (itself a loosely defined term) and
purchasing habits.

The purpose of measuring the ROI is to be sure that the
community is beneficial to the organization. It is possible to
measure the returns of the community as a financial value
(or a range of financial values).

ROI Error 2 — Trying to use a single formula

Many conferences, books, and other literature have been devoted to creating a single ROI framework through which all

communities can be measured. This assumes that all communities are created for the same goals or achieve the same returns for the organization.

The problem is that different organizations create different communities for different reasons. It is not possible to accurately compare a community started to generate feedback on products against a community started to generate new sales leads. There is no single formula to measure all fans or all activity within a community.

ROI Error 3 — The precision problem

Many practitioners oppose the ROI process due to claims of inaccuracy. These claims carry some validity. It is difficult, for example, to measure whether a lurker reading comments in a community later saw a product in a store and, based upon what they had read, purchased the product.

In this case, tracking only direct sales through the community (or tracking cookies) would understate the benefit of the community. Tracking growth in the community against increase in sales would include a broad range of activity that may not be attributable to the community.

What if a community provides an organization with a terrific product idea that later becomes a best-selling product—how can this be measured? Does the community receive the credit for all profits generated by that product? What about the marketing/PR effort that promoted and sold the product? What about the research and development to make it a reality?

What about referrals from existing community members? How can the quantity and quality of referrals from existing members accurately be reflected in the ROI of the community? How can a community manager accurately predict the future benefits of the community?

There is a difference between precision and accuracy. Precision is a cause of frustration and a significant loss of time. It will leave you only measuring the things that are easy to measure (usually direct clicks through the platform). The goal is to be accurate; to have a defensible methodology based upon verifiable data.

ROI Error 4 — Using biased metrics

Many studies claim that every Facebook fan is buying x% more than a non-fan of a product. This figure is then used to extrapolate the value of the page by multiplying the percentage difference between fans/non-fans by the value of the product. For example, a member of the Coca-Cola fan page purchases 27% more than a non-fan or an extra $75 per fan. The return of this page, with 43 million fans, is approximately $3.225 billion.

This is an erroneous conclusion. Sales of Coca-Cola have not increased by $3.225 billion. In addition, it's clear on Facebook that only a tiny percentage of fans actually receive updates from the page. But the fundamental flaw in this methodology is confusing correlation with causation.

Causation is where a change in one variable is responsible for changes in another. For example, customers buying more of a product is a cause of higher profits.

Correlation is where two variables change in relation with each other but not necessarily because one caused the other. Many mistakes are made at this stage. For example, in the Coca-Cola example, did being a fan of the Facebook page cause people to purchase more Coca-Cola? Possibly. Let's not rule this out entirely. But it is more likely that those who buy more of the product or service *already* are bigger customers of the product/service and are more likely to join the Facebook fan page.

Therefore, being members of the page didn't cause people to purchase more. It is important in our calculations to control both for members vs. non-members, and use the increase/decrease in spending of non-members to ascertain how much of the increase/decrease of members is attributable to the community.

A related problem is confusing the benefits of the medium with the message. In 2008, Dell revealed they were earning several million dollars a year by selling discounted products through Twitter. Many social media advocates claimed this proved Dell had an ROI of several million by Twitter.

Yet by this logic, we can claim the phone made Dell billions of dollars. We cannot attribute sales to the medium. Offering discounts through any channel is likely to gain sales (and there is a big difference between revenue and profits, especially on discounted products). The brand, the products, and the price play a bigger role than the channel.

Simply converting your biggest customers into community members does not allow you to attribute their sales to the community. It might transfer sales from one medium to another, but not increase those sales. You cannot compare members with non-members. You need to show that these very people are now purchasing more as a *result* of being members of the community.

RULES FOR MEASURING ROI

Some simple ways to measure the ROI are by using the three rules below, which fit the very definition of ROI:

1. **A return is a financial metric, which means either increased revenue or decreased costs.** Any non-financial metric (e.g. engagement) is not included in the ROI.

2. **An investment is a financial metric of cost incurred.** Any non-financial metric is not applicable.

3. **A return must be directly attributable to the investment.** Correlation is not causation. A return must be directly connected to the investment. For a return to be included, you must be able to prove that it is the result of the investment.

These three rules exclude many of the metrics highlighted in the academic material—activity within the community, loyalty, engagement, and search rankings. Unless you can reliably connect them to community activities (e.g. community increases search ranking by (x), (x) improvements led to 10% increased sales since this occurred), exclude them from the formula.

Other values such as insight and innovation are not directly attributable to the investment. Do not include them as part of the ROI formula (you can add them as footnotes for your clients' consideration).

You know by now that a community can offer several direct returns to an organization:

- Increased spending from existing customers
- Acquisition of new customers/new business
- Reduced costs
- Increased productivity
- Fulfillment of the organization's mission

Measuring increased spending per customer

Increased spending per customer might be achieved through a combination of the following:

1. **Increased purchases of existing products/services.** When individuals are connected together, their interest in the topic intensifies. This often means they participate in the activity/

topic more often and thus purchase more of that product/ service.

2. **Increased retention rates.** Members of a community have a higher level of loyalty towards the product and service. As a result, they're likely to continue purchasing the product/ service when non-community members might leave. Remember that you're not tracking loyalty, you're tracking retention.

3. **Customers purchasing new products/services.** Through the community, members might learn about newly available products/services and purchase them. They might purchase more premium-level products and services to keep up with others in the group.

4. **Advertising revenue.** As a result of more members actively participating in the community, the community may earn more money from advertisers or attract new advertisers. This is highly relevant in online communities for news/media organizations.

Calculating these returns is complicated and not immediately verifiable from a single source of data. Many organizations only calculate direct, trackable, sales that are generated from the community. This excludes the psychological impact of the community upon purchasing habits. Most of the benefits are lost.

For example, by participating in a community a member might increase their loyalty to the product and subscribe directly to receive it. So you need to ascertain two statistics: the increased number of sales attributable to the community and the number of *active* members in the community.

To measure this data you need to know four things:

1. **Spending of non-members.** For example, imagine Apple releases a new iPhone. Both members of Apple communities and non-members are likely to purchase it. Unless you know the number of non-members who purchase the phone, you would attribute all the sales to the community and not the

product. You need to use non-members as a control group so you know what spending occurred only among members.

2. **Spending of newcomers to the community.** People who join the community are likely to be those that purchase most frequently from the organization. You cannot fairly compare active members against non-members. That's simply transferring sales from one medium to the next. However, by comparing the spending of active members to newcomers, you can find out whether that spending increased (or decreased) since joining the community.

3. **Spending of active members.** Measure the spending of active members to compare against the newcomers in the community. This shows whether active members spend more than newcomers to the community. While newcomers may already be better customers, by looking at the difference between newcomers and active, you can see whether spending increased since they joined the community.

   This figure alone isn't enough. Spending might have increased due to factors that are unrelated to the community (the release of a new product, for example). Remove the increase/decrease in the non-members group from this figure, which isn't attributable to the community.

   Multiply the average by the number of active members in the community to identify the value of active members.

4. **Spending of lurkers in the community.** Lurkers may also offer a return. They might not participate, but by visiting the community, consuming information, and sharing it elsewhere, they become more likely to purchase from the organization. To identify whether this is true, use the same process as active members.

   First identify the average spending levels of lurkers and subtract the spending level of newcomers to reveal whether lurkers spend more than newcomers. Then subtract the spending increase in non-members during this same period and multiply the average increase in spending per lurker by the number of lurkers in the community.

The following spreadsheet illustrates how to calculate these figures:

	Spring 10	Summer 10	Autumn 10	Winter 10	Spring 11
Increase/decrease in purchases					
- non-members	61	44	58	32	73
- total value of prev. quarter purchases	$7,015.00	$5,054.00	$5,760.00	$3,686.00	$8,141.00
- avg. value of non-members quarter	$115.00	$114.86	$99.31	$115.19	$111.52
- avg. increase/decrease in spending per quarter	$8.00	-$0.14	-$15.55	$15.88	-$3.67
- newcomers sampled	113	107	213	154	113
- total value of prev. quarter. purchases	$18,645	$16,505	$34,550	$25,773	$16,549
- avg. quarter value of member pre-community	$165.00	$154.25	$162.21	$167.36	$146.45
- active members sampled	57	41	83	77	64
- total value of prev. quarter. purchases	10659	7534	15345	16993	13289
- avg. quarter value of member post-community	$187.00	$183.76	$184.88	$220.69	$207.64
- avg. quarter increase/decrease in spending	$22.00	$29.50	$22.67	$53.33	$61.19
- avg quarter increase/decrease attributable to community	$14.00	$29.64	$38.23	$37.45	$64.86
- # active members in the community	995	1138	1245	1195	1099
- est. value of active members	$13,930	$33,730	$47,592	$44,758	$71,277
- lurkers sampled	32	19	42	35	43
- total value of quarter purchases	5560	3215	8326	6623	8105
- avg. quarter value of lurkers	$173.75	$169.21	$198.24	$189.23	$188.49
- avg. quarter increase/decrease in spending	$8.75	$14.96	$36.03	$21.87	$42.04
# lurkers in the community					
- # members visited within the past month	1903	1857	1967	1922	1897
- # members which made a contribution within past month	1138	1245	1195	1212	1107
- est. # of lurkers	765	612	772	710	790
- est. quarter increase/decrease attributable to community	$0.75	$15.09	$51.58	$5.99	$45.70
- est. value of lurkers	$574	$9,238	$39,823	$4,256	$36,106
Total increase/decrease in spending attributable to community	$14,504	$42,968	$87,415	$49,013	$107,383

Spending spreadsheet

Collect information on purchasing habits

Spending levels are best collected through direct data. This is relatively easy when members use the same e-mail address for purchases as they do for the community. You can simply compare the e-mail purchases against community member-ship to see before and after purchase habits.

When this is not possible, you can survey members and use self-reported spending within the previous year/quarter. Per quarter is preferred because members are more likely to accurately report spending per quarter as opposed to per year.

Measuring increased retention rates

To measure the increase in retention rates attributable to the community, use a similar process.

First identify the average retention rates of non-members, newcomers to the community, active members, and lurkers directly from company records.

Once you have this data, subtract the newcomer retention rate from the active and lurker rates to reveal the increase (or decrease) in average retention rates per individual since members have joined the community. Then subtract the increase or decrease from non-members from both of these figures (active members and lurkers) to control for elements that are not attributable to the community. If the retention rates of non-members increase, for example, you need to subtract this increase from any increase in the community.

This provides an average increase or decrease in retention rates that is attributable to the community. Now you need to know the value of retention. This will vary per customer or employee. For an employee, it might involve the training costs for new staff, or productivity lost during staff transition. For a customer, it will be the average profit per customer.

Retaining a high-spending customer (a likely community member) is worth more than a low-spending customer.

Once you have this figure, multiply it by the number of active community members and lurkers to gain a value for retention.

Note that this figure should not be combined with the increase in purchases, which would duplicate the figures significantly. Retention must be its own objective for the community.

Measuring purchases of new products/services

Customers who purchase new products or services will include this amount within what they spend at the organization (you also control for this by accounting for non-members).

So you are already tracking members purchasing new products/services. The only addition you might make is asking members to be more specific about what products/services they purchase.

Measuring advertising

If your community generates money from advertising, include this figure as money generated from existing members. Advertising revenue is a figure that is directly gained from the advertiser/invoices/advertising data package. If you are using pay per views, pay per click, or pay per action campaigns, you can get this data directly from the analytics package.

Measuring new customers through community

A community can attract new customers, clients, or business to an organization through sales leads, word-of-mouth activity, or other business development opportunities.

Measuring new customers is easier to measure than an increase in retention rates.

Measuring sales generated from community leads

By establishing a community, an organization may be able to identify and capitalize upon sales opportunities. This is most common in small, exclusive, communities with a high-value client base. Many organizations in the healthcare sector have highly-targeted communities of pharmaceutical buyers each worth $100,000+ a year in their organization.

By connecting with these individuals and understanding their problems, the organization might identify sales opportunities to win new business.

This must be new business, and not customers transferring from one medium to the next. You need to measure sales generated from community leads (for example, by keeping track of '*how did you hear about us?*'). Deduct the cost of sales to reveal a profit per sale. Then multiply by the number of sales to reveal a figure for sales generated through the community.

In larger communities this may prove difficult. You might need to use a proxy figure, such as profit from sales generated per week (and multiplied by 52, the number of weeks in a year).

Attract new customers	Spring 10	Summer 10	Autumn 10	Winter 10	Spring 11
- Sales leads generated from community	3	7	13	4	7
- total of sales attributed to leads from community	$40,772	$81,237	$210,445	$72,336	$134,565
- Less costs of sale	$21,554	$50,293	$93,401	$28,738	$51,374
- profit from sales generated by community	$19,218	$30,944	$117,044	$43,598	$83,191
Profits from events	$0	$0	$0	$0	$0
Sponsorship profits	$0	$0	$17,000	$17,000	$17,000
Focus groups/Research	$0	$0	$0	$0	$0
- misc	$0	$0	$0	$0	$0
Total additional revenue generated from new business	$19,218	$30,944	$134,044	$60,598	$100,191

New customer revenue

Measuring miscellaneous revenue

The community may present a variety of business development opportunities (sponsorship, events, merchandise, focus groups) that has otherwise not been considered. The community itself may become a direct source of revenue through a membership fee.

This can usually be directly measured and included within your data.

Measuring cost reductions, productivity improvements, and . . . 'happiness'

By developing a community, an organization can *reduce* a number of costs, including:

- **Advertising/marketing/PR.** If an increasing number of the target audience is participating in an online community, less money needs to be spent in other channels to reach them.

- **Customer service.** If members are now turning to the online community to answer their questions, it may be possible to reduce the customer service costs. This is direct income attributable to a decrease in staff.

- **Recruitment costs.** If an organization is recruiting individuals from online communities (e.g. StackOverflow), this may lead to a direct decrease in costs that would usually be spent on recruitment or headhunters.

These costs (returns) are derived directly from the source (e.g. finance team, marketing team, customer service team, or recruitment). Note that a cost saving is a not a singular occurrence, but a continual metric. The returns of cost-savings can increase exponentially. You need to track the cumulative cost reductions.

For example, if an organization sets up a community to reduce customer service costs, you need to measure the current customer service costs and any reductions in these costs *attributable to the community*.

Assume there are six members of the team, earning a combined $110,000 per quarter. If more people go to the community to ask questions and receive support, it may then be possible to reduce the staff. If one person becomes part-time as a result, the spending would then be $105,000 per quarter. This is an ongoing saving; $20,000 in the first year, $40,000 within the second year.

Repeat this process for marketing/PR/advertising costs. Measure any on-going savings that can be attributed to the community. Note this accounts for transferring of budgets from one medium to the next by including the investment.

You can also calculate the average cost of a recruitment agency/headhunter and savings made as a result of hiring individuals through the community. This may also include any job advertisement costs saved by promoting the position through the community.

Cost Reductions	Spring 10	Summer 10	Autumn 10	Winter 10	Spring 11
Reduced customer service costs					
- total spending on customer service team	$110,000	$105,000	$105,000	$99,500	$99,500
- Savings		$5,000	$5,000	$10,500	$10,500
Cumulative savings		$5,000	$10,000	$20,500	$31,000
Reduced marketing spend					
- total spending on customer service team	$275,000	$265,000	$265,000	$257,500	$240,000
- savings		$10,000	$10,000	$17,500	$35,000
Cumulative savings		$10,000	$20,000	$37,500	$72,500
avg. recruitment costs	$5,350	$5,350	$5,350	$5,350	$5,350
# members hired through community	3	1	0	1	3
Savings	$16,050	$5,350	$0	$5,350	$16,050
Cumulative savings		$21,400	$21,400	$26,750	$42,800
Total reduction in costs	$16,050	$20,350	$15,000	$33,350	$61,550
Cumulative reduction in costs	$16,050	$36,400	$51,400	$84,750	$146,300

Cost reductions

Increased productivity

Be aware that a community can increase the productivity of staff members through staff sharing knowledge, resources, best practices, collaborating more effectively with each other, or simply through an increase in morale.

Measuring productivity is more complicated than other metrics. The best measure to use is the profit per employee in the community against profit per employee not in the community. If this is difficult to calculate, then use a percentage measure of individuals in the community and percentage of non-members, against the increase or decrease in the productivity ratios over this time.

You can then attribute a proportionate percentage to the community. To be validated, the increased productivity should correlate closely with growth of the community.

Fulfillment of organization's mission

For non-profit organizations, a community may often serve no other purpose than to directly support the organization's mission. A community for those affected by cancer, for example, is not designed to increase revenue but to serve the fundamental mission of the organization.

It is possible to put a theoretical value upon this. For example, you can use a satisfaction/well-being score (from surveys) divided by the costs of a community, as opposed to cost of other activities. But unless the community leads to a cost reduction in other channels (which is possible), do not include it as part of your ROI calculations.

THE COSTS/INVESTMENT OF COMMUNITY

The costs of a community include everything necessary for the community to be developed. This covers three categories.

1. **Fixed costs.** These are the one-time costs to launch a community: consultancy, platform development, internal training, etc.

2. **Ongoing resource costs.** Maintenance of platform, software licensing fees, hosting, advertising, etc.

3. **Ongoing labor costs.** The community management, a percentage of time from other staff members (e.g. management, marketing, etc.).

These costs are best obtained directly from the source. In some organizations, only the total budget will be available. It is useful to break these costs down into the categories listed here to reveal whether the community is likely to generate an ROI in the future.

This sample spreadsheet outlines costs:

Ongoing costs (quarterly)	Spring 10	Summer 10	Autumn 10	Winter 10	Spring 11
Resources					
Media creation	$0	$0	$0	$0	$0
Advertising	$0	$0	$0	$15,000	$0
Hosting	$570	$2,400	$2,400	$2,400	$2,400
Development	$1,500	$1,500	$2,500	$3,500	$1,500
Software licensing fees	$17,000	$17,000	$23,000	$27,500	$27,500
Labour					
Community management	$15,000	$15,000	$19,500	$19,500	$19,500
Content creation (if excl. cmgr)	$0	$0	$0	$1,100	$0
Internal IT (if excl. cmgr)	$2,000	$2,000	$2,000	$2,000	$2,000
Internal marketing (if excl cmgr)	$0	$0	$3,500	$3,500	$3,500
Ongoing marketing campaigns	$0	$0	$0	$0	$0
Total ongoing costs (quarterly)	$36,070	$37,900	$52,900	$74,500	$56,400
Total costs	$149,570	$300,970	$467,370	$655,370	$825,270

Cost figures

Also calculated above are the cumulative costs (total costs) of the community thus far. You need this figure to measure the ROI of the community.

Calculating the ROI of the online community

Once you have calculated the returns generated from the community, and the investment made in the community to date, it is relatively simple to calculate the ROI of the community.

The ROI = (return – investment) / investment

First calculate the cumulative costs and returns of the community.

Returns	Spring 10	Summer 10	Autumn 10	Winter 10	Spring 11
Increased business	$14,504	$42,968	$87,415	$49,013	$107,383
New customers	$19,218	$30,944	$134,044	$60,598	$100,191
Cost savings	$16,050	$20,350	$15,000	$33,350	$61,550
Cumulative costs of the community	$149,570	$300,970	$467,370	$655,370	$825,270
Cumulative returns of the community	$49,772	$144,034	$380,494	$523,455	$792,580
Cumulative Profit/Loss	-$99,798	-$156,936	-$86,876	-$131,915	-$32,690
ROI	-67%	-52%	-19%	-20%	-4%

ROI

In this example, the cumulative cost of the community is $825,270; the cumulative return of the community is $792,580.

Therefore, the profit of the community is -$32,690. The ROI is therefore, -$32,690 / $825,270 = -4%

Although a negative ROI, this minus figure fails to reveal whether the community's ROI is increasing or decreasing.

Trends over time

By reviewing and graphically displaying the trends of costs and returns over time, you can see which direction the community is heading (and the speed at which it is heading in that direction). The previous example would look like this:

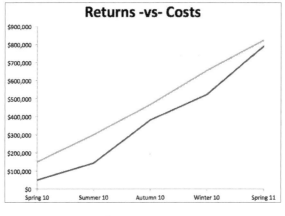

Returns vs costs

The graph on the following page shows that although the community's ROI is negative, it is rapidly catching up to the costs and should soon surpass the costs. Despite a momentary blip, there is no reason to suspect that the community will not shortly achieve a positive ROI.

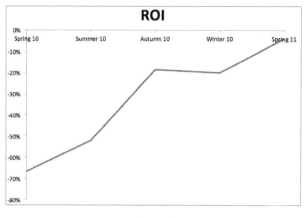

ROI graph

ROI per active member

An organization that has invested heavily in an expensive website, a promotional campaign and support/consultancy, may find the community has failed to generate a positive return within the first year and cancel the project.

But single costs like those detailed above are unlikely to be incurred again (at least within the next few years). If these are no longer on-going costs, it may be highly beneficial to the organization to continue the community as the cost of acquiring more members is low and the benefits high.

Marginal cost of one extra member

You need to know the marginal costs and benefits of acquiring additional members by dividing the number of active members in the community by the variable costs (staff costs + developer costs + miscellaneous expenses) to acquire them.

This will provide a cost per active member of the community—how much it costs to attract and keep a member highly engaged in the community. This metric can also be used to assess the ability of community managers.

Marginal benefit of one extra member

Now you need to identify the marginal benefit of each extra member of the community—the return of each extra member of the community.

To understand the benefit per active member, you want to know the total returns of the community as highlighted above divided by the number of active members in the community. This will provide a useful average.

ROI per active member

If you subtract the cost of each extra member by the benefit, you have an ROI per active member. For example, if it costs $5 to keep an active member in the community, and the benefit is $7, each member generates $2 in profit for the community.

The profit / by the investment ($2/$5) gives you your ROI percentage = 40%

Essentially, for every dollar an organization spends on the community from now on, they could expect to receive $1.40 in return. This figure is likely to be higher than they would receive through most other channels of investment. Therefore, it would make sense to continue the community.

Including overheads

Of course one-off, sunk costs recur again every few years. Websites often need to be redeveloped or adjusted to account for technology changes, changing user habits, best practices, or an array of other reasons (including the whims of executives).

This cost is difficult to estimate. For your purposes, divide the cost of the previous platform by the average number of years between community platform redesigns/changes (four years).

Then treat this as a variable cost that is included in the marginal cost of one additional member.

Lurkers again

For lurkers, you can calculate the average ROI per member, and then multiply this figure by the number of active members.

Footnotes to the ROI

A number of other direct financial benefits violate the rule that a benefit must be directly attributable to the investment.

These include:

- **Benefits of new products ideas/innovation.** An online community can lead to new product ideas, research, or innovation that may become bestselling products. It is not feasible to attribute the entire profit of this product/service to the community effort.

  The research and development cost to turn the idea into a reality, the marketing cost, the distribution and a number of other facts are also responsible for its success. For this, however, we provide a range by comparing against the average of previous products/services and then examining the difference in profit.

  Yet, this too, fails to account for a particularly innovative marketing campaign or an extensive sales push.

- **Improved performance of staff recruited through the community.** Staff recruited through the community may be of higher quality/talent than staff recruitment through other channels. It is not easy to attach a figure to this increased performance. We can use anecdotal measures of anything notable the staff has achieved and place a range of value upon that.

- **Long-term impacts of the community.** This also fails to account for the future value of the community. Community costs are traditionally front-loaded, they incur more significant investment at launch than they do over time. Therefore, the ROI is often understated in the first two years (or proved to be a negative ROI). Without understanding the ROI trends, it is easy to conclude a community does not yield a positive ROI.

- **Any off-line referrals as a result of the increased sense of community.** It is not possible to track any off-line referrals as a result of the community. While we believe that increased community activity is likely to lead to increased word-of-mouth activity, there is no clear study that links the two. Therefore, we are not able to track this.

None of these are sufficient reasons not to measure a community. They appear as notes below the ROI calculation. They should be taken into consideration when making decisions about investing further or decreasing costs in the community.

## CHAPTER 9

User Experience

You can work on your website's user experience full-time—or ignore it entirely. These two extremes reflect the fact that the task is never complete. User experience can always be improved. Some community managers prefer to focus on tweaking the website, while others skip it altogether. Neither is the right approach.

I suggest you allocate a fixed amount of time each month to improving the user experience. Choose specific aspects of the experience you will enhance. The time you spend on each task should be based upon where you are in the community lifecycle.

In the early stages, optimizing the user experience won't be as important. You don't have many members, so you need to interact directly with them. In the maturity stage, the user experience should take up a lot of your time. Your tweaks will have a big impact upon the many people in your community.

IT'S YOUR JOB TO IMPROVE THE USER EXPERIENCE.
Don't leave the community website to someone else. I've seen too many community managers wash their hands of the user experience, claiming they don't know what to change or how to change it, or they think they don't have the power to change it.

My suggestion? Learn about user experience. Plenty of great sites and books can help you. Learn how to test an intervention to improve the user experience. Work hard for the power to make the changes. This is one of those things worth fighting for.

Don't detract with new platforms

One worrying trend in recent years is for community managers to create an account on every new social media platform that appears. Many communities now have links to Facebook, Twitter, LinkedIn, Google+, Quora, Instagram, and others.

Before you consider doing this, identify the benefits. Take Google+ for example. If you have to tell your audience to add your Google+ page to get the fan base, what benefit does it have? You're essentially spreading yourself across more platforms without attracting any additional members to the community. Remember social density? You want the level of social density to be high. If you have 30 members talking on Google+, 59 on Twitter, and 79 on Facebook, you've spread the activity very thin. As a rule, unless you're going to tap into members you don't already have, it's usually better not to bother with new social media platforms. If you have to promote the platform to your existing audience, all you're doing is dissipating activity.

Instead, the community manager should be looking at ways to simplify and optimize the technology. You should make it easier to use the technology.

You may, for example, be developing a mobile-friendly version of the website or refine features that haven't received much use. The goal of improving the user experience is to focus on elements that ultimately increase the number of interactions between members on the platform.

A number of measurable steps lead to interaction. For example, the processes by which people navigate through the site, the positioning of elements on the homepage, and the amount of data shown next to each discussion topic.

You want to identify the link between every single step and ensure it's as smooth as possible. This usually means removing or repositioning elements rather than adding new elements.

Never forget that the purpose of the community platform is to facilitate interactions within the community. It serves the same purpose as a community meeting hall; it brings people together and encourages them to interact. Any element that doesn't encourage this should be removed.

Simplify, simplify, simplify. For example, that big graphic on your homepage that welcomes newcomers to the community—how many of your visitors are newcomers? Probably not many compared with your regular members. Yet your regular members repeatedly see the same message, which isn't even designed for them. This doesn't encourage activity. Why not remove it?

How about your blog feature? How many members write blogs? In most communities it's something that the organization wants members to do rather than what members are doing. You can probably remove this too.

GUIDELINES FOR OPTIMIZING USER EXPERIENCE

A basic rule of thumb is to make a large number of small iterative changes as opposed to major redesigns. Members are usually resentful of new platform designs. They protest that their base has been affected. They might calm down over time, but the outrage can affect the long-term affection that members have towards the community.

If you do need to make a major change, then be sure to involve members at a very early stage. Show them what it's going to look like, seek their frequent opinions on the changes (and adapt the changes accordingly!).

Refine the most used features

It's better to spend more time refining the features lots of members already see and use than to develop new features no members will use.

Small refinements on discussion boards, notifications, layout/design, and profiles yield much better results than adding in a new feature. For example, tweaking how signatures appear can have a profound impact upon the community. Likewise, making the anti-spam system more efficient can also significantly improve the number of interactions in the community.

Look to the most popular elements of the community platforms (the most popular pages and features), and see where some small tweaks might have a huge impact upon the community. When testing, either use a parallel comparison (so the feature changes for a segment of the users), or a time comparison (the previous week versus this week).

Look for statistically significant data (in proportion to the total sample). Failing that, usually an increase/decrease of 10% or more indicates useful information.

Even the most minor things, like changing the space between forum discussion comments, the type of font used, the size of the font or the way the messages are displayed from the homepage can have a big impact.

You might, for example, rename the categories for clarity or to provoke curiosity. Focusing on the tweaks that will have an impact upon the overwhelming majority of your members is a great use of your time.

Remove, don't add, features

If you begin with the goal of figuring what to add, you'll never optimize the site, and you'll waste a lot of time and money.

It's usually better to remove text, elements that aren't used, pages with low traffic, and so forth.

If you have blogs, picture sharing, befriending, private messaging, separate wall profiles, discussions, and shoutboxes, it diffuses the level of activity from members into many different areas. This makes it more difficult to follow any single part of the website, and the additional choices lower the level of activity among the entire community.

You should measure which features aren't being used and remove them.

Highlight the popular stuff

Rank things by popularity. Put the most popular forum discussions first. List the most popular pages nearer the top. The more you highlight what's popular, the more activity you will get.

The homepage—that first page members reach when they visit the community—should show what's popular in the community at any particular time.

List the pages of your community by the number of page views. Remove those that aren't viewed very often from any navigation menu or position them below the more popular pages on the navigation menu.

Respond to what members do, not what they say

There is a big gap between what members say and what they do. They ask for features that they might not use. They complain about things that don't affect their levels of participation in the community.

Fortunately, you can track what members do, their actions and activity.

See what members are using and build a feature for that

It is also important to see what members are doing with the tools provided. If they are sharing pictures or stories through the forum, it would make sense to add a specific feature for that in the community.

In the WarriorCats community, members use the forum as a chat room. It would make more sense for WarriorCats to add a chat room. The goal is to respond to the community and cater to what members are doing more than what they are saying.

WarriorCats

Test and measure

Before you make any change in your community website, benchmark where you are now. Make a reasonable hypothesis about what you expect to improve. Then measure whether your change has had the desired effect.

The more data you collect, the more accurate you will be. Comparing one day against the previous day isn't effective. Comparing the same day one week against a similar day the next is better. But it's best to compare weeks and months against each other. Be careful, however. November will trump December (Christmas holidays). Summer months are usually a little less active. Just be sure to measure like for like.

Notifications

Notifications are an essential feature of community platforms. Notifications affect every member.

The notification is an e-mail that people receive when someone has responded to their contribution. It's short, direct and includes a link to the discussion/activity. These affect every member.

Notifications are essential to community development. They let members know that they have received a response to their contribution to the community. This encourages them to return to read this response and respond in kind.

We call this the notification cycle. The notification cycle helps keep members engaged in the community. Newcomers who make their first contribution enter the notification cycle whereby they are continually updated about responses to contributions. They visit, respond, and other members are thus notified.

It's very difficult to build a successful community that doesn't have notifications as an opt-out feature. This opt-out feature is important. It means that members are automatically informed about new updates to their contribution unless they decide to turn this feature off.

Most members don't change the default settings. If the default setting is opt-in (members have to elect to receive notifications), few members will change this. As a result the community will struggle to sustain high levels of engagement. If the notifications are opt-out, the levels of engagement are typically much higher. Members can opt out if they feel they are receiving too many notifications.

The typical options include real-time updates, daily updates, or no updates. Real-time is ideal, but can be overwhelming for highly active members. Once a day sounds good, but in practice people ignore e-mails that are received at the same time every day.

You can shorten the message, change the text, tweak the subject line, change the 'from' field. Each of these can have a significant effect upon whether someone opens the notification, clicks the link, and decides to opt in or out of the community. Over a period of time you should be able to optimize these.

Notifications can be measured. You should be able to test the impact of notifications, which type of notifications work best, and most importantly, how to optimize the content of the e-mail itself to increase the number of people that click the link.

Homepage

The design of the community platform matters a lot. Many organizations make very similar mistakes. They limit the number of interactions on the platform. You should apply best practices and test variations of community website design.

The most important element is the homepage—the first page members see when they visit the community domain. In some communities, newcomers see a slightly different page than members.

Some organizations make the mistake of tailoring their homepage to newcomers. Here the page reads like a sales/promotional advertising. It might include a large welcoming graphic, promotional material, a paragraph explaining what the community is about.

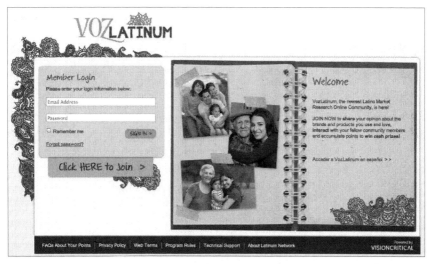

Voz Latinum

The recently launched Voz Latinum community appeals to newcomers at the expense of regular visitors. This reduces the number of visitors to the community platform. Without showing the latest activity, there is little motivation for members to join.

This is a mistake for several reasons. Search engine traffic is not a high source of new members; few newcomers visit the homepage without knowing what the community is about. The homepage is primarily visited by existing members, not newcomers. It should be aimed at existing members.

Most members will visit a specific discussion or be referred by a friend or a link elsewhere. These members already know what the community is about and simply need to see a lot of activity they can participate in.

The homepage should be a snapshot of everything that's new in a community at any given moment. Mumsnet, SK-Gaming, and MyGarden are great examples of this rule in action.

Key elements of the homepage

- **Latest news: content produced by the organization and community volunteers.** The organization should publish at least one news post a day. The latest news should be featured on the community homepage.

- **Latest contributions made by members on forums and elsewhere.** People get a sense of efficacy when their posts appear here moments after they publish them. It encourages instant gratification and quick replies from others. Don't include information that's irrelevant to the majority of your members such as 'Fred has added Jane as a friend.'

- **What's popular?** This shows members what others are doing in the community right now. It guides them in their own discussions and highlights activity. Knowing what's popular helps bond the community around common themes.

- **Who's new?** Showcasing members who have joined encourages existing members to say hi. It increases the conversion ratio of newcomers into regulars—others have taken an interest in them.

- **Who's popular?** This can take many forms (featured member, interview, rankings, etc.) but showing which members are most popular at any given time provides others with people to emulate. They might also want that level of attention and popularity, and participate more frequently to get it.

- **What's needed?** Have a list on the homepage showing members what they should do right now, whether it's to add their opinion on a topical debate, submit their questions to an upcoming guest VIP, or otherwise make a contribution to the community.

- **Notifications/replies.** In a top bar, highlight the notifications members have received to comments they have posted. These are actions that need the member's attention.

The Student Room platform is an excellent example of a community that combines most of these elements. Newcomers are immediately greeted with a number of discussions and activities they can participate in. Regular members can see, at a glance, what's new in the community.

The Student Room

Ensure the latest activity is above the fold. Typically 'latest activity' is filled with friend requests, comments on profiles and other boring information. Try displaying the latest discussions and upcoming events above the fold.

Change the copy

You can try changing the tone of the copy. Remove redundant words. Use shorter, punchy, sentences. Remove paragraphs that aren't necessary. You can make the copy more or less formal to suit the personality of your target audience. This might be more sarcastic or humorous, or, perhaps for communities of practice, more formal and dry.

Community of Sweden

The Community of Sweden (above) uses far too much copy, which clogs up the forum page: an explanation of the forum, descriptions about each category, and a large tag cloud. None of this is necessary. People intuitively know what a forum is and myths about Sweden is a self-explanatory category. This is also true for the other category headlines.

Change the colors and design

Make small, tiny, changes in the color and design of the website. Try using a smaller number of colors. Ensure the design emphasizes things that members most want to do in the community; below is a good example.

My Garden

Show unanswered posts

Have an option to show the latest posts on the community homepage. Encourage and challenge members to answer these especially tough questions.

Remove threading (or add single threading)

Most online communities revolve primarily around a forum-based discussion platform. If you respond to a post, it appears indented next to the contribution you're responding to. This makes it easier to follow the exchange on that particular topic.

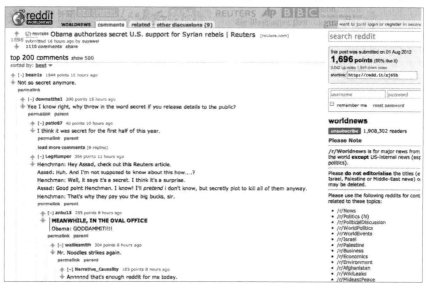

Reddit Deep Threading

Reddit uses deep-threading. People reply to individual responses and not just the main post.

Threading is a classic example of a simple, powerful, optimization. However, it also presents a dilemma. Threading makes it more difficult to follow the discussion in its entirety. As a result the number of discussions may shrink as people find it more difficult to follow the discussion. Numerous sub-threads can evolve from a single thread.

Community managers are faced with several options. The first is to have no threading. Each new response appears in chronological order beneath the discussion above. This is the most traditional approach to threading and is still very popular today (some platforms do not allow deep threading).

The second is to have one-deep threading where single discussions relevant to a comment are indented below that comment but don't allow any deeper discussions than that. This is currently popular as a best of both worlds approach.

The third and final option is to enable deep threading up to a limit (after too many indents, discussions will be off the page). This usually allows up to five indents.

So which is best? I don't know. At present there is no published data to suggest any approach yields any unique benefit. My experience favors no threading as the approach that yields the highest number of interactions. Others adamantly support deep-threading.

Therefore, you need to test threading choices yourself. You can do this in one of several ways. First, enable deep threading, one-deep threading, and no threading for a single week and track the number of interactions between members. This is the best approach, but be careful of the dates themselves skewing the results. For example, if one week includes a national holiday, the number of interactions will be significantly lower.

The second approach is to allow certain categories or discussions to use deep-threading, some to use one-deep threading, and others to use no threading, then see what works best.

Integration

Improve the integration with social media platforms. Have popular discussions posted to followers on Facebook/Twitter/Google+ with a question and a link to where they can participate. Ensure tweets mentioning the topic appear on the community site.

Automation

Automatically deactivate inactive member accounts (with a reminder). Welcome new members with a responsive series of e-mails that reflect their action (*After your fifth post we recommend you …*). Improve the feature to retrieve lost passwords. Congratulate members on milestones achieved. Close old discussions after three months.

Reputation

If the community has been going for a while, consider embracing a reputation system. A reputation system encourages people to actively share what they know to increase or maintain their reputation within the community.

Member profiles

Ask more interesting questions in the profile page e.g. *Where were you when you heard Michael Jackson died?* Ask questions that other members will be keen to click on the profile to find out the answer. Have a funny default image until members change it.

FAQ

Add the most common questions in the FAQ, not only the site, or the community's history, but about the topic in general. Make this an incredibly useful document that people want to read.

Go mobile, maybe

Most communities have discovered a rise in visits from mobile devices that correlates closely with the use of these devices. So it's tempting to develop a mobile version of the community platform for these users.

Mobile presents both an opportunity and a dilemma. A mobile version of the site is only useful when it increases the number of interactions on the platform. If people are accessing the mobile version of the site and participating perfectly fine at the moment, will a mobile-friendly community platform increase the number of contributions? The answer to this question depends heavily upon two factors:

- **Are mobile users participating less?**

  It's no use just tracking the number of visits from mobile users against other users. You need to track whether those who participate from mobile device are participating less.

  People might participate less solely because they have less time to participate. They're on the move after all (and using a device not suited to typing). However, the platform may make it more difficult to participate on a mobile device. In this situation, a mobile version of the site would increase the number of interactions on the platform.

  If there is little difference between the number of contributions as a percentage of mobile users compared with traditional visitors, a mobile version probably won't help much.

- **Are there habits hampering mobile users that could be resolved by a mobile-friendly version of the platform?**

  Another question to address is whether there are things that the mobile user isn't doing in the community (which other members do) that have a negative impact upon people overall in the community. Mobile users, for example, may spend less time writing blog posts, reading content, and watching videos, but more time sharing pictures when on the move, responding to single discussions, voting in topical polls, etc.

You might also consider a mobile version of the site but only if it will increase the amount of activity from mobile users.

Lifecycle optimization

The best way to identify things that might work in your community is to look at other top websites and see what they have done.

But be mindful that community websites need different features at different stages of the lifecycle. A community should launch with relatively few features and gradually expand from there. Only imitate a community in the same stage of the lifecycle.

Finally, remember that optimizing the user experience is an on-going process, not a one-time task. Prioritize which elements you're going to optimize (perhaps one a month), and gradually test to see what works best. Dedicate a certain amount of time to it (perhaps five hours a month) and then stick to a schedule.

WEBSITE EXAMPLES

Some examples of websites I like include:

- The Student Room: http://www.thestudentroom.co.uk
- RockandRollTribe: http://rockandrolltribe.com
- Lenovo: http://forums.lenovo.com
- Element14: http://www.element14.com/community/index.jspa
- Backyard Chickens: http://www.backyardchickens.com

These sites aren't the prettiest, but they're very effective at facilitating interactions between members.

## PART TWO

Everything You Need to Know About Your Members

In 2009, FeverBee landed our biggest client yet. The prominent company sold a well-known product within the B2C sector that half of you probably use. With a large budget, they had launched their community, ran a huge promotional campaign, hired a small team to manage the community, and recruited one of the world's top legal firms to write the terms and conditions for the site. They had thrown everything possible at the community, and it still wasn't taking off.

They had a large number of registered members, but few active participants. They had tried stimulating a number of discussions, activities, and created a lot of content, but the level of response would be a brief spike at best.

Our diagnosis showed two problems. The first was they had the wrong strategy. They had fallen victim to *big launch syndrome*. They had tried to gain a lot of attention within a short amount of time, which is fixable. The second problem was more difficult: the organization had created precisely the type of community its target audience had no interest in participating in.

To turn this community into a success, they had to start again. They had to redo what they had already done. They had to entirely rethink what it was about, who they were targeting, how they were positioning the community. We showed them all the research that supported our statements. We had surveys, interviews, and a lot of data all diligently collected.

...and they agreed, but then said it was impossible to change it. Six months after we stopped working with them, the community platform vanished and hasn't reappeared since.

It's much easier to do the research before you launch the community. Research is the quickest shortcut to develop a successful community. It tells you exactly what type of community to create, how to create it, and what actions you need to take within the community.

Some of this is obvious. You need to know what platforms your members use before deciding what platform to use, for example.

Some of this is less obvious. You need to know what issues your members really care about. You use these issues to initiate discussions and stimulate interesting content. You need to know what members aspire to do and be. Then you can build a community concept on helping members turn aspirations into reality.

You need to know what your members already know, and what they want to know. In *Cultivating Communities of Practice* (2003) Etienne Wenger called this the *Domain of Knowledge* and it defines what members talk about. You need to know the edges of this knowledge.

For example, imagine you run a community for street dancers. As part of the audience analysis, you ask about their aspirations. You ask what they know and what they want to know. Through a series of interviews, you identify some common trends. Many want to form a local crew (dancing group), appear on a music video or appear as a supporting act at a local gig *(I'm guessing, I have no idea what street dancers want—I haven't done the research)*.

Now you can plan discussions, activities, and content around these desires.

YOU MIGHT INITIATE DISCUSSIONS SUCH AS:
- What are your top tips for getting gigs at local clubs?
- How many of you have recorded a video?
- How did you find your crew members?

YOU MIGHT ORGANIZE EVENTS SUCH AS:
- Live discussion: What do local clubs want?

YOU MIGHT CREATE CONTENT SUCH AS:
- 10 members share their stories of finding and growing their crew.
- The member-created 'how to record your first video' guide.

You might also tweak the community to ensure it personifies the concept: a community of street dancers looking to earn a living, or create their own videos, or find crew members.

This concept is the position statement of the community. It distinguishes the community from others in its field. If your community is entering a mature field, you need to do this. You need to have a unique position that established communities cannot cater towards.

In addition, you might recruit volunteers to take responsibility for reflecting these aspirations with relevant content and discussions.

One volunteer might be responsible for writing regular tips about recording videos, interviewing members on the topic, hosting activities/online workshops about it, and otherwise ensuring your community is the best source of interactions on the topic.

You can take it further. You could work with your top members to develop a course for members to achieve their goals. You can earn money here *and* help your members get what they want.

There is no shortage of opportunities. The important step is to understand what members want and know how to take that information and apply it to practical activities within the community.

Too many communities launch and then struggle to grow their audience, attract members and sustain high levels of participation. Either they got the concept wrong and couldn't attract the audience in the first place, or they couldn't keep members engaged once they did arrive.

The audience and sector analysis is the solution to these problems. Many community managers do analyze their audience, but it's too superficial. They rely solely upon social media monitoring tools such as Radian6. While these tools are great for monitoring, they are far from comprehensive. They can reveal the number of times topics are mentioned and even sentiment towards those topics, but they won't tell you the aspirations of members, their habits, nor what their biggest challenges are.

Proper analysis may involve these somewhat superficial tools, but also more professional research techniques including in-depth interviews, surveys, and research of relevant media.

A true and thorough analysis goes much deeper than messages shared on social platforms. They uncover the real motivations, hopes and aspirations of the audience. They identify the shared experiences and symbols of your audience.

They reveal terrific data you can use to conceptualize your community and engage your members.

You need to undertake an analysis that covers three main areas:

1. **The community's interest sector.** Every community lives within an ecosystem (sector). It is therefore important to have a thorough understanding of that sector. This reveals how to position the community and make it relevant to your members. For those with existing communities, it shows how to make the community more relevant to members.

2. **The individual's actions and attributes.** You need to know who your audience is and what they do. This will help you use practical platforms, promotional strategies, content strategies and develop an overall plan to get the community started.

3. **What the target audience thinks and feels.** This is the most important; you want to know what your audience really cares about. This will help you attract members and retain their interest. You need to know about their experiences, hopes and ambitions, and their biggest challenges. What provokes a significant emotional response?

THE BUBBLE FALLACY

Many brands build communities around concepts that are entirely irrelevant to the audience they're trying to reach.

Brands (or those who work for brands) live in their own bubble. They see the brand as very important because they must: they work for it. Whenever they see the brand mentioned elsewhere, it confirms what they believe.

What they don't realize is that for the audience they're trying to reach, the brand is usually only a tiny part of their lives. If you try to build a community around a brand that is only a tiny part of their lives, you will probably fail.

The majority of communities that fail right now do so because they haven't properly conceptualized. They haven't properly reviewed what their audience is really interested in. They build their community about themselves, and not about the audience they're trying to reach. Can you see what this means? Most of the new communities built by organizations are doomed before they have begun.

With data, they would have identified who the audience is, what the audience wants, what issues most interest the audience, what communities exist already, and then built a community around that. But most organizations don't do that.

This is why you see communities for a particular type of diaper as opposed to a community about parenting, or a community about a DIY shop as opposed to a community about DIY work. The Home Depot Community (below) is about DIY projects, not about Home Depot.

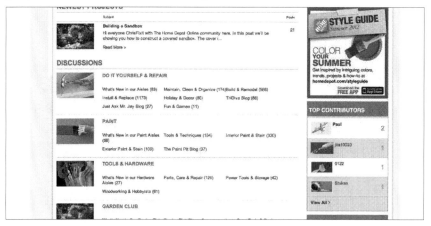

DIY Community

If you properly collect and analyze data, you will know how to build a community that's much more relevant to the lives of the audience you're trying to reach.

CHAPTER 10

The Community Ecosystem

Every online community lives within an ecosystem. Even a community that defines its ecosystem is still encompassed within it. For example, *PlanetJitsu* is a community for JuJitsu enthusiasts, and it's within the JuJitsu ecosystem. Changes in the JuJitsu ecosystem would affect the community. Hence you would need to fully understand the JuJitsu ecosystem.

PlanetJitsu

To make matters more confusing, a community can exist in more than one ecosystem. Any significant changes to the entire martial arts ecosystem affects the JuJitsu ecosystem and the PlanetJitsu online community.

To build a relevant, robust community requires an analysis of five areas: issues, media, people, competition and trends.

I will cover each of these in depth, beginning with the key issues within the ecosystem.

Issues

An issue is a singular matter of attention. Issues can only exist with a concerned audience. Without that concerned audience, there is no issue (as an aside, this is why it's easier to build communities around existing issues rather than fabricating new ones).

Issues encourage interactions and unite groups of people who hold similar opinions. They provide people with a reason to interact with each other. They become signifiers for those visiting the community for the first time. Issues make up much of what we talk about.

There are a near-infinite number of issues within any given sector. A community benefits by understanding the most widely held issues within any sector and bringing these issues into the community.

Many communities can even capitalize on and take over the issue within the confines of that community. Mumsnet, for example, doesn't just discuss the issues of sexualization of young children through clothing and ads, but it leads on the issue with its *Let girls be girls* campaign.

Mumsnet

There are four types of issues you want to know about within your sector.

1. **The biggest issues at present.** At any given time there are many issues within the sector. In the golf sector, Tiger Woods's affairs and subsequent poor performance on the course were the biggest issues for a period of time. These can be identified by mentions in mainstream media or frequency of mentions on social media platforms.

2. **Controversial issues.** Some issues are naturally more controversial than others. Politics and religion are usually contentious issues, yet in most communities, there is usually something specific that divides members. Who or what is the lightning rod issue that divides people interested in that topic? In golf, it might be gender bias, or golf players turning professional at too young an age.

3. **New issues/rising issues.** What are the new issues that are gaining attention? They might not be the biggest yet, but they are new and relevant. These issues will usually be on the cusp of political, economic, societal, or technological changes. For example, in golf, a growing number of people are calling for the belly putter to be banned.

4. **Emotive issues.** This is similar to controversy but with a range of emotions beyond the negative. Some issues might generate pleasure and excitement. You need to know which issues these are. They might be related to upcoming events, products, or realization of goals. For golf, it could be an upcoming tournament, the prospect of the next champion, or the release of a new club.

Considerable overlap between these issues is fine. The goal here isn't to correctly categorize the major issues, but to identify them. Once you identify them, you can use them in your community development activities.

Identifying issues in the ecosystem

There are several ways to identify the four types of issues.

First, you can review relevant media within that sector. Most magazines, for example, highlight the major issues on the front cover. It is possible to order back copies of magazines at three-month intervals for a period of years. This will reveal which issues have longevity and which provoke fierce controversy.

Golf Monthly

Alternatively, most publications now have websites with a

search feature. It is a relatively simple task to skim through these websites and identify the major issues within the sector (it is even possible to search for 'controversy', 'anger', and other emotive words to find the trending issues).

Another useful tool is Google Trends to identify and compare various issues into a simple ranking.

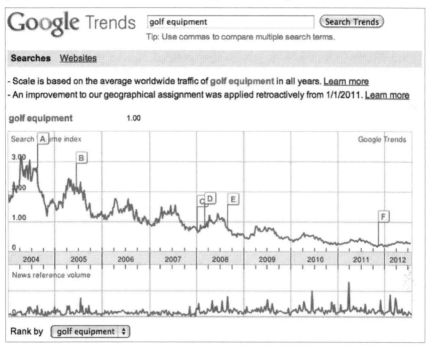

Google Trends

Second, you can identify the major blogs in the sector and review what they are discussing. Blogs usually cover the most popular issues at any given time, so a blog search will reveal which issues are relatively new and will soon reach mainstream. Alltop.com cites the top blogs on a variety of topics.

Alltop

Most sectors have lists of connected blogs. If you're struggling to identify the major blogs, try searching for terms such as top 10 (topic) blogs. You can also ask members of your target audience what blogs they believe are popular.

Third, you should visit existing communities that are relevant to their niche. You should review the forum topics or discussions to see which issues are gaining popularity. You may also review Twitter discussions to see what people are tweeting.

All forum topics			Create new thread
Topics	**Threads**	**Posts**	**Latest Post**
New to the forum? Welcome. Please introduce yourself to others passionate about golf	1013	7411	26/07/2012 at 22:25
General Get it off your chest!	13376	308337	Today at 20:55
Charity Golf Days Put your game to a good cause. Ideas, experiences and challenges	58	254	30/07/2012 at 09:32
Magic action Video sequences of you and your favourites	189	2199	Yesterday at 17:43
Golf instruction Slicing, hooking, shanking, topping? You name it, GM members will have a cure	3589	46828	Today at 20:59
Golf equipment What's new, what's good, what's bad. Everyone has an opinion	12387	148314	Today at 19:35
Golf courses Where to play? The beauties and the beasts	2318	21614	Yesterday at 17:28

Golf Forums

Social media monitoring platforms can also be utilized at this stage. These can reveal the major issues being discussed in a variety of communities. But they should not be used as an all-purpose tool.

By the end of this process you should have a list of the biggest, newest, most emotive, and most controversial issues. You can use this list to conceptualize the community and develop the right discussions, content, and activities for your audience.

## CHAPTER 11

Competition: Existing Online Communities

It is important, both before and after a community has been developed, that any existing online communities, mailing groups and social gatherings within the same ecosystem are identified.

It would be a mistake to launch a community to compete directly against this competition. You need to know what niche they fill, what areas they don't cover, and what percentage of the audience they have.

Specifically, you need to know:

- What are the most successful communities within that sector?
- What type of communities are they?
- How old are the existing online communities?
- How active are they?

IDENTIFYING EXISTING COMMUNITIES

There are several ways to identify existing communities. First, directly ask the target audience which communities they participate in and are aware of. Second, search for communities via search engines.

Do not only search for (topic) community, but also (topic) forum, (topic) fans, (topic) groups.

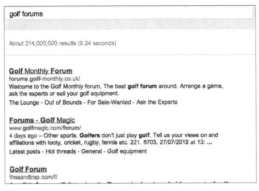

Google Search

What happens if no such communities exist? This presents either a major opportunity that a niche hasn't been filled or a major warning that there is not a strong enough common interest to create this community. It's usually the latter.

Identifying existing community 'type'

Communities can be classified in several different ways. One popular method is to classify a community by its purpose: leisure, relationships, causes, self-improvement and collaboration.

The problem with this method is it doesn't quite cover the full range of communities and not all communities have a defined purpose. Many communities are simply where people come to chat about things that are of interest to them. The members of IndieTalk, for example, have no broader community purpose but just wish to talk about independent films.

Some classify communities by the platform; for example, social networks, message boards, chat rooms, virtual worlds, and so forth. But that's a redundant way to actually help develop a community. Tools facilitate communities but they're not communities by themselves.

The best way to classify communities is not by purpose or platform but by the strong common interest that unites the community. Every community falls within one of five different categories:

1. **Communities of interest.** By far the most common type of online community is the community of interest. These are communities of people who share the same specific interest. It might be television shows (The Bronze), a love of rare coins (CoinTalk) or a fondness for swords (Sword Forum). People join communities of interest to share their love of a specific topic with others.

2. **Communities of place.** These are communities based on geography. The people in the local neighborhood, perhaps, or those who live in London or expats. These are the most well-known types of communities. Increasingly many online communities are being created for geographically close members. Good examples include EastDulwich, W14, Harringay Online, Townepost (Indianapolis).

3. **Communities of practice.** These communities are comprised of members who undertake the same activities. One example is a community based upon a profession. Another is a community that engages in a common sport, craft, or business. ShootingPeople is a thriving community for filmmakers. Lawyers.com is for lawyers.

4. **Communities of action.** Communities of action are dedicated to making change in the world. This includes most of the non-profit and political community efforts. Increasingly, many other types of communities evolve into more of an activist force about their topic over a period of time. The Family Guy community (Damn You all, among others) has saved the show on several occasions. The Unofficial Greenpeace community is highly active too. The likes of MoveOn, Kiva, and Avaaz are all communities of action.

5. **Communities of circumstance.** People who are within a circumstance not of their own making include most health communities, LGBT groups, and others with a common self-interest. These communities are often very strong

but difficult for an organization to create. MacMillan has a thriving community for those affected by cancer.

Many online communities overlap in several of these categories and this is a positive aspect of a community. As a broad rule, the more categories a community fits in to, the stronger the common ground of the members. For example, the Geneva Web Communications community is both a community of practice and a community of place.

A community that fits into more than one category targets people with a greater number of shared interests. They might both live in the same location and participate in the same profession (as in Geneva Web Communications), or they might be teachers who want to transform teaching such as TeachForAll Synergies (practice and action).

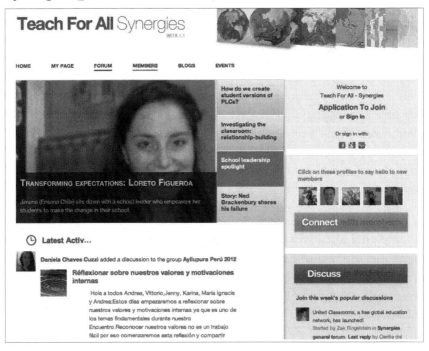

TeachForAll Synergies

The (intentionally) absent category

There is no community of products/services. This category doesn't exist. For a community to succeed, the product/service needs to be positioned within one of the other categories. You can develop a community for iPhones, for example, because the audience has a strong *interest* in the product. In reality, few products are interesting enough to develop a community around.

Identifying existing community age

There are several ways to identify the age of the community. The most common are:

1. **Review when the domain name was registered.** Type the URL into (domain name registrant), click for more info (or WHOIS), and see when it was registered.

Whois registration

2. **Scroll to the earliest forum posts.** You can usually save time by changing the number at the end of the URL of the second page.

3. **Look at archive.org for that internet address.** Archive.org will usefully show you how the community developed over a period of time.

Identifying community size

It is not always easy to identify the size of a community. Many forum-based communities show the number of members and active members at the bottom of the page.

Others, such as Ning, reveal the total member count when you click on members.

What's Going On?
Currently Active Users
There are currently 269 users online. 76 members and 193 guests
Most users ever online was 402, 14-Jun-2012 at 20:37.
A1ex, Achilles, Alex1975, alnecosse, AmandaJR, backwoodsman, Bomber69, BTatHome, Carbon, Chrimbo, chris661, CliveW, Deke, DelB, derm, Doon frae Troon, doublebogey7, drive4show, FairwayDodger, ForeRighty, fundy, gregk2, GreiginFife, groundskeeperwilly, GTO NEMESIS, HawkeyeMS, Heidi, Hobbit, Hodgie, HomerJSimpson, laing, lmurg, Jack991, Jungle, Junior, jwm, Jws63, karlcole, Kurt92, Largsgolf1974, leaney, Midnight, Moff, Neddy, NorfolkShaun, Phil2511, PNWokingham, Pro Zach, Pull, RichardC, rickg, rmcin626, Rooter, SammmeBee, Sandy, Scottjd1, sev112, Shiny, Slab, Slicer30, slicer79, steve1133, SwingsitlikeHogan, thecraw, timchump, Toad, triple_bogey, Valentino, wookie
Today's Birthdays
jimbo (69), Captain_Black (52), Y5Stu (43), BigBoppa (37), rockshot07 (36)
Golf Monthly Forum Statistics
Threads: 43,443 Posts: 629,949 Members: 14,888
Welcome to our newest member, shammay

Golf Monthly Stats

Occasionally, the URL of individual members will reveal the order in which they registered, i.e. a person might be the 17,215th member to register. In that case, you can visit the newcomer thread, click on a recent newcomer, and have a good idea of how many people have registered for the community.

Growing/stable/in decline

You want to know whether the community is growing in activity, is relatively stable, or is in a decline. One way of identifying this is to use archive.org and compare the growth/decline of activity in the community over a one-month period.

You can subtract the total post count from one month to the next and divide this by the number of days between to obtain the number of posts per day. You can then repeat this process for a subsequent month/year to ascertain the growth of the community.

A simpler way is to use Alexa traffic as a proxy for activity. While this doesn't show whether the community is more active, it will show whether the number of people visiting this URL has increased/declined during a given period.

Platform

You also want to know what platform the community uses. This is directly useful when developing or refining your own community efforts. You can usually identify the platform by reviewing the source code (Chrome > View > Developer > View Source).

```
<!--[if IE]><![endif]-->

<meta http-equiv="Content-Type" content="text/html; charset=UT
<meta id="e_vb_meta_bburl" name="vb_meta_bburl" content="http://www.thestudentroom.co.uk" />
<script type="text/javascript">var NREUMQ=NREUMQ||[];NRE      push(["mark","firstbyte",new
Date().getTime()]);</script>
<base href="http://www.thestudentroom.co.uk/" />      if IE]></base><![endif]-->
<meta name="generator" content="vBulletin 4.1.8

<link rel="Shortcut Icon" href="http://static2.tsrfiles.co.uk/1.63.6/cpstyles/tsr-
blue/images/custom/favicon.ico" type="image/x-icon" />
```

Source code

Most platforms will be based upon forum packages, white label social networks, or enterprise platforms. A few will be entirely custom community platforms so won't appear to show a well-known package. In that case, simply list the community platform as "custom."

Finally, you want to identify anything that could be relevant to the success of that community. This might be a unique design, its top members, the culture/personality of the community, the types of conversations, or the involvement of its founder.

MEDIA ANALYSIS

An organization should be cultivating a positive relationship with relevant media on behalf of the community. This allows the organization to release messages, promote the community, attract new audiences and increase the status of audience members.

Organizations should undertake a comprehensive media analysis of relevant media. This analysis should identify:

1. The top publications in that sector
2. The top journalists in that sector
3. The top bloggers in that sector (AllTop.com, Technorati and other sites can help here)
4. The top influencers in that sector
5. The format of popular stories in the sector

The top publications in that sector may not always be found in a newsstand. Further research will be needed to identify the key publications. At most, this will involve searching for (topic) magazines.

The top bloggers in the sector can be identified through a variety of websites, such as AllTop, Technorati, social media tools or by Google searches for blogs in that sector. Look for "top 10 (topic) blogs," as in many sectors there are bigger blogs. Look towards the comments on the blog or Feedburner numbers to identify the number of readers.

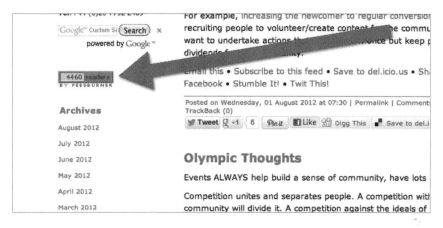

Feedburner

Specifically, you want to know who is writing stories relevant to the sector in various media channels, how they can be approached, what format their stories appear in and what they have covered in the past.

When reviewing a magazine, for example, you might identify a regular Q&A column, a 'day in the life of' section or a 'top 10 tips' section that might be able to feature something relevant to the community.

INFLUENTIAL PEOPLE AND ORGANIZATIONS

The final piece of the sector puzzle is to identify its power players, the most influential community members. The media channels mentioned above often write about them.

Tiger Woods, for example, is a major influencer within golfing communities. The CEOs and managing directors of major golf manufacturers, tournaments and player organizations are also key influencers.

You want to know who has power/influence within your sector. Who are the people that attract attention? Who are the people that can make major changes within that sector?

There are several different sorts of influence, including:

1. **Fame.** Those who, for whatever reason, are the most known within the industry, for either positive or negative reasons. They might have high levels of charisma or character traits that attract notoriety.

2. **Power.** Those who through their position and authority wield significant influence within the sector. They will usually be CEO or high-ranking individuals.

3. **Expertise/skill.** The individuals who have a higher level of skill and/or expertise than others. They are able to use that skill/expertise to create change within that sector.

4. **Relationships.** Individuals who wield influence due to their relationships with others. They may be connected to others listed above and be able to leverage those relationships.

This list should encompass every key person of note within the community's sector. You will use the list in several ways for your community. First, it will be the source of topical news and discussions. As you will learn, people like to read about, and discuss, other people.

Second, it will be a key source of interviews, guest posts, live-discussions and expert opinions on topical issues. You want to build close relationships with many members of this list so they will support the community (and receive publicity/attention within it).

Third, those on this list will be able to endorse the community, provide exclusive insights and otherwise attract more people to join and visit the community. They may also be able to support the community in creating new business opportunities or other development activities.

## CHAPTER 12

The Audience: Demographics, Habits, and Psychographics

Now that you have a complete picture of your sector, you need to understand your target audience: who they are, what they do, and what they think.

This information will inform all future community development activities. It will guide how you structure the community platform, the activities you host for the community, the discussions you initiate, who you reach out to and how you sustain high levels of activity.

Location

The location of your members is relevant when creating content, developing sub-groups, developing communities of place/interest, arranging meet-ups, or initiating relevant discussions.

For many communities, the location reflects general population statistics and is spread evenly across the nation. For a few, there may well be opportunities to use concentrated numbers of people to develop the community. Certainly potential members of a NASCAR community are more likely to be based in the southern USA than in the north.

The best way to identify location is from an organization's own records or by an analysis of its existing web traffic—especially to those areas which show a heightened interest in the organization/topic (e.g. company history page). For example, analyzing the location of visitors from social media platforms or news stories.

Google Analytics and Alexa both provide a good location overview of visitors to any given website. You may also use social media platforms to get a member's self-identified location.

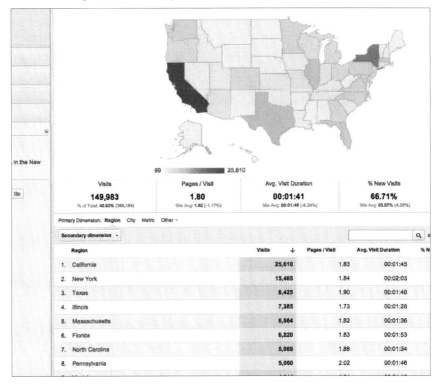

Analytics

Again, it is important to remember that precision is not the goal. The numbers do not have to be precise; they merely have to provide the *insights* you need for your later activities.

You want to identify *clusters* of people. If you have a large number of members from Cleveland, it might make sense to treat them as a potential sub-group you can target and bring to the community in a single effort. You might even want to start the community solely with one large cluster and expand gradually once you have established momentum.

Age and gender

Most organizations should already know the age/gender and socio-economic class of their audience. For the organizations that do not, this information should be compiled either from existing records or from a survey to those who already visit the site.

Classified Sales Manager

Rob Edwards (020 3148 2512)

Key Facts

Frequency:	Monthly
Circulation:	60,130 (ABC Jul-Dec 11)
Readership:	468,000 (NRS Jan-Dec 11)
Target Market:	ABC1 men aged 25-54

Rate Card

Full Page Rate: £4,633

Advertising information

One way to gather this information is to look at magazines that target this audience and request their advertising material. Alternatively, look at who advertises to this audience and analyze who their target audience might be. This is often stated on corporate literature.

Profession

If the organization's community is job-related (communities of practice, for example), it is useful to have an understanding of the job titles of members of your organization.

This can be gathered from a survey of the audience (those who complete the survey will be the first invited to become founding members of the community) or from reviewing 20 to 30 LinkedIn pages from a random sample of target members. In some sectors, it is also possible to randomly sample a few members by e-mail address and use a search engine to identify their professions.

AUDIENCE HABITS: WHAT ARE MEMBERS DOING?
Now that you know who your audience are, you need to know what they do. You need to know both their online and offline habits. Specifically you need to know what they do online, what internet tools they use, what they read, what they do in their spare time, and when they are usually online.

Each answer is essential to creating a practical community development plan and ensuring the community remains relevant to an audience's experiences. Ultimately, the community serves to improve the lives of its members. You need to know as much as possible about the current lives of members to achieve this.

For example, if later you want to increase the sense of pride that members feel, it helps to be featured on websites members read. If you want to host events in the community, you need to know when they access the site and browse the internet. This also reveals, for example, whether your competition is other leisure activities, work, or something else.

The sector analysis you've already done might reveal some information about this audience; however, you are likely to need a survey to get all the information.

Specifically you should ask:

• **What tools and platforms do members use? This will guide your community site development process.** You will use the tools members are most familiar with. This should be a multiple-choice question.

- **What does the audience read online? This will guide your promotional activities, your status-enhancing activities and your relationship activities.** This should be a multiple-choice question along with space to add their own reading materials.

- **What aspects of the topic are the audience most interested in? What sustains the attention of your audience? What topics make the audience emotive?**

- **What time do they browse the internet? This should be a pure multiple-choice question.** You want to know what period of time. Is it the morning before work, is it at lunch, is it during work or in the evenings? How late will they be online? Do they go online much at weekends? You can also gain this information for existing communities by reviewing Google Analytics.

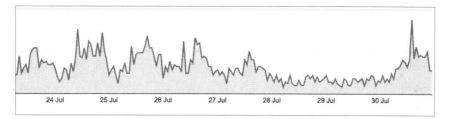

Visits by time of day

- **Specifics of habits related to the topic.** When do people participate in the topic, for how long, what specific aspects of the topic do they participate in? What are their processes for participating in the topic?

From this data, several common themes should emerge. For example, we might find golfers use Twitter to follow the top players and talk about their latest putting scores. They read golf magazines, but not blogs. They're most interested in equipment and ways to be better at golf, and they browse the internet after work and family time from 9pm to 11pm.

We might also find they play golf at the weekend, they prefer to go to golf courses close to home but do occasionally travel to a golf course on holiday, most of them have been playing golf for more than five years, but there is a sizable newcomer group.

List these themes in each category in order of popularity. Be careful not to incur a selection bias when doing the survey. It would be foolish, for example, to ask members via Facebook to take the survey—the majority of members will note they use Facebook at the same time the survey was advertised (you would be surprised how often this happens!).

AUDIENCE PSYCHOGRAPHICS

Finally, you want to know what the audience thinks and feels. This is more important than you might imagine. Most positioning efforts for a community are based upon psychographics, not demographics. An organization has to thoroughly understand the individuals it is trying to reach. This helps in segmenting the target audience and conceptualizing the community.

Psychographics are commonly researched through the Interest, Activities, and Opinion (IAO) variable framework. Others embrace a wider framework that includes the target audience's attitudes and values.

For the purposes of online community research, learning the attitudes and values of a target audience is unnecessary. Semantic definitions vary and interpreting an audience member's remark and attributing it to an underlying value is subjective. Mainly, however, community managers don't work at the values and attitude level. A community manager does not change someone's values or attitudes. Community managers identify what people are interested in and build a community around those interests.

The challenge isn't in persuading members to be interested in what you tell them, but to pinpoint that interest as specifically as possible.

Therefore you want to identify not just the broad interest *"I like golf!"* but the specific nature of that interest *"I want to improve my golf handicap to impress my boss and get that promotion!"* You could easily build an entire community concept around this.

Collecting audience psychographics

It is not possible to gain this psychographic information from surveys and observational analysis. Psychographics analysis requires interviewing individual members of the target audience.

Contact five to 10 potential or existing members and schedule interviews with them. These should not last any more than 15 minutes. The longer the interview lasts, the more willing participants will be to say anything to end the interview. So keep interviews short and sweet.

During these interviews you need to ask them how they became interested in the topic, their fondest memories, what their lives are like, what they are worried about, what they would love to see within that topic in the future, thoughts on topical issues and other pertinent questions. (*See "Questions For Your Audience" on page 272 for specific questions.*) Further probing should be done in areas that could yield more precise insights.

If someone claims he's interested in golf equipment, probe further. Is he interested in the putter? The club? Is he looking for quality equipment at an affordable price or the best quality equipment regardless of price?

From these—recorded!—interviews you should create transcripts and color-code them according to the challenges, experiences, and aspirations. From this information you will be able to uncover and aggregate key data that you need to develop the community.

You also want to identify the *specific phrases* they use. Ramit Sethi refers to this as the *mindreading technique*. You can later echo back to the entire audience the specific phrases members use.

This process should also highlight prospective community members who are likely to want to be one of the first members once the platform is launched. The final interview question should be, "*Would you like to be one of the founders of the community?*"

Symbols

Try to identify symbols from these interviews. Symbols are words, images, ideas, and anything else that have a specific meaning to this target audience. Element14 is a common element used heavily by its target audience (design engineers) to create their products. The community for Element14 is quite literally a symbol.

These symbols play an important role in developing a successful online community. Symbols are clear identifiers that the community has been created specifically for this specific audience. Rock and Roll Tribe has clear symbols throughout its website. The tagline memorably reads, "*Fuck middle age—let's rock.*" I think you would agree that's a pretty clear positioning statement for the target audience.

Rock and Roll Tribe

If you want your community to appear less as a covert marketing attempt and more as a genuine approach to connect likeminded people, it's important to identify and use these symbols. Identify the expressions members use when describing the topic, identify words/phrases that have specific meaning to them.

In my video gaming communities, there were so many symbols it was difficult to keep track. For example, to *slayer* meant to score o points in a game. Slayer was the game name of a somewhat arrogant player who once publicly scored o points. To outsiders, this expression was meaningless. To insiders, it telegraphed this community was for them.

QUESTIONS FOR YOUR AUDIENCE

Biggest problems/challenges

- What key issues do they care about?
- What are they struggling with?
- What are they worried about?
- What interests members? What do they mention without being prompted?

Experiences (successes, failures)

- How did they become interested in the topic?
- What is their average day like?
- What have been their biggest achievements/failures?

Aspirations

- What are their hopes, fears and aspirations?
- What are their commonly held symbols within the field?
- What language do they use when discussing the topic?

APPLYING THE DATA

As I mentioned earlier, if you're creating a community (or struggling with an existing community), you can apply this data directly to the community concept.

The first stage of launching a community is conceptualization. At this stage your data influences the key decisions you have to make. These include the following:

Who is the short and long-term target audience?

A community should not target its entire possible audience upon launch. It should instead target a small segment with as much homogeneity as possible. By understanding the audience analysis, you can segment your audience by demographics, habits, or psychographics (who your group are, what they do, or what they think). This means to begin with, you target a group of individuals who share as many demographic, habits, or psychographic attributes as possible.

When you begin the community, you can target all activities solely for this group. This increases the likelihood of the community reaching a critical mass of activity. Ideally, you use two or more qualifiers e.g. a community for (x) who (x), a community *for industrial designers* in *London*, for example, or a community for industrial designers passionate about renewable materials.

The greater the level of homogeneity between members, the more likely it will attract the specific target audience. Facebook launched as a social network for Harvard students, then it became a social network for students in the USA, then the world. It was not until *two years* after launch that everyone could join the community.

You can expand later, but in the beginning you just need to reach critical mass. Segmenting the target audience will help you achieve this.

Your early activities in the community are highly influenced by its focus. If you develop a community for industrial engineers in London you can initiate discussions about the London area, jobs in London, individuals in London. By catering solely to this audience, you're more likely to attract this audience.

What type of community (place, practice, interest, action, circumstance)?

Now that you know the target audience of the community, you need to know what type of community you will create. Don't underestimate the importance of this. A community of action is very different from a community of interest. A community of circumstance is not the same as a community of practice.

This will affect what content you create, the people you invite, the activities/events you host, the benefit members get from the community, and how you moderate the community.

Most organizations default to developing a community of interest about either the organization or its products, yet this is the hardest type of community to create. There are very few products (or organizations) that we're interested in enough to spend our spare time talking about. In many cases, it would be far better to develop a community of action, or a community of place.

TeachForAll Synergies is a good example of this. There are many established communities for teachers out there. Rather than create another community of practice, they instead have decided to create a community of action, a community that wants to change something in the world.

If your data shows you that a large number of members feel there is something wrong that they would love to change but don't know how, this is a great opportunity to create a community of action around that challenge. This doesn't solely have to be non-profit communities. People who buy green products might believe in a broader green cause. People who buy productivity tools might believe in productivity education for children.

The type of community you create should be informed by the data you have collected. For example, if you've noticed the target audience is clustered around a certain location, it would make sense to develop a community of place.

As I mentioned, the type of community changes everything. Let's quickly review.

- **A community of interest usually discusses the most interesting things about the topic.** This can be good or bad. People exchange their history, views, and passion on those interesting things.

- **A community of place usually talks about what's happening locally.** They talk about events, relevant issues that affect them and how they can improve the local area. They also work together to share advice about the area.

- **A community of practice typically helps members to become better at what they practice.** They share advice and tips. They often provide something of a support groups for members.

- **A community of action is devoted to change.** They establish or highlight goals and milestones and explain to members what they need to do to help the group achieve those goals.

- **A community of circumstance typically focuses upon experiences and bonding.** Members share their pain and help each other through it. They might also provide advice/support.

Whichever type of community you choose to create will entirely influence what happens in the community. This naturally leads into the positioning of the community against others in the sector.

What is the positioning of the community?

If you're launching a community into an ecosystem with several established communities, it is important to differentiate it. In their classic book on positioning, Jack Trout and Al Ries stress the importance of being the only category in its field.

The same is true for communities. Your new community should be the only community of its kind. It should not compete against established communities. Competitors might enter the fray later, but you were first and attain the advantages that come with being first.

Look at the battle of social networks throughout the last decade. Friendster dropped the ball and MySpace dominated the audience. Facebook couldn't compete, so instead launched the first student-only social network. LinkedIn launched as a business/professional social network.

You can't compete head-on with established communities. Your community has to be a different *type* of community or it needs to have a unique focus, benefit, or personality. Let's imagine you want to launch a community for teachers. That's a competitive field. There are lots of existing communities for teachers.

You might instead develop a community of place for teachers who live in the UK, like TESConnect.

TESConnect

You might develop an exclusive community for history teachers (community of practice). How about a community of teachers who love new technology (community of interest)? Or like TeachForAll Synergies, you might develop a community for teachers trying to change the profession (community of action). You might launch a community for teachers suffering from stress or depression (community of circumstance).

This often means you need to begin with an exclusive community (or at least exclude a big chunk of the potential audience to get the community going). You might launch an exclusive community tailored to only those who meet narrower criteria. The community should attract people for a different reason than other communities.

The mistake many organizations make is trying to make the community superior through better technology features. This never works because members don't move from one community to the next because it looks better, or it offers technology that others don't. What makes a community different is its focus and personality. The positioning problem cannot be solved with mere technological features.

It is important therefore to carefully review the existing communities and position your community accordingly. If your community is struggling to gain traction within its ecosystem, it may require repositioning.

What are the objectives/benefit of the community?

People usually join a community for a clear benefit and link that benefit to the reason they initially participate—for example, to satisfy their information needs. Over time, their social motivations (need to belong, achieve things, etc.) take over (Kraut and Ren, 2008).

It's important then to properly articulate the benefit of the community. A community for lawyers '*to connect*' isn't as powerful as a community for lawyers to grow their own practice or master a specific skill set. It's useful to use the data gathered from your aspiration survey and align it with the key benefit of the community.

Be careful not to *solely* cater to information needs, which can attract information-seekers (commonly known as lurkers).

What will members do in the community?

The final piece of the conceptualization puzzle is what members will do in the community. Will they participate in events/ activities? Will they interact with each other?

You can use the data collected on audience habits, psychographics, and analysis of other communities to identify what activities are likely to be popular. By activities, I am referring to the types of discussions, content, and outcomes that members are most likely to respond to.

For example, if you're developing a community of action your discussions should revolve around actions that further the cause. Your content will be about upcoming actions or progress, or the contributions of members.

An ongoing, rigorous, process

It's important to have a rigorous process for collecting your data. However, you need to know how to apply it. In Part One, I explained how this data informs *all* your community management activities.

The audience analysis, however, is not a one-time event; it is a continuous, ongoing, process and you should do it every six to 12 months to ensure the community remains as relevant to its target audience as possible.

Community Management Success

The time has come for community management to emerge from the dark ages and become a professional discipline. However, for it to become a discipline requires . . . discipline. It's no longer enough to visit your community and react to it. You need to be proactive. You need to avidly collect and analyze your data.

You need a professional approach that embraces the data you have available. This data is your biggest friend. It tells you exactly what's going on in your community. You need to use data to identify what your community needs and then make that happen.

Using data, you can improve every single aspect of community management. You can test and refine your approach. You can be sure that you're using your time as effectively as possible, that your work will have the biggest long-term impact upon the community.

Community managers should be rated based upon their data. They should be able to prove how valuable they are. The best will rise to the top. The weakest will make excuses. They will hide their data and get defensive when asked about growth, engagement, sense of community, or ROI.

This is good news for great community managers. As the community management role continues to grow, I hope that the ad hoc approach many take now is gradually phased out in favor of a professional approach.

I hope that community managers endeavor to continually develop, not merely maintain, their communities. I hope that organizations realize that there is a big gap between the skills of an amateur community manager and a professional.

In short, you need to love your data. You need to constantly collect it. You need to master the theory that underpins your work and know how to apply it. Data isn't something to be left to the end of the year; it's a continual process that lies at the heart of successful community management.

Recommended Websites

The Bronze http://bronzebeta.com

Sadly this community appears a little lost now that the Buffyverse has died down. Still, considering the show ended almost a decade ago, it's been an incredible example of a community of practice.

CoinTalk http://www.cointalk.com

I love this as a simple community of interest. People come to discuss and share their love of coins. Peter Davis has demonstrated just how important the fundamentals are. Simple platform, great management, strong common interest—if you get these wrong, you tend to struggle.

Damn You All http://www.damnyouall.net

Family Guy fans. In fact, very active Family Guy fans. These are the sort of fans that save their show, not bemoan its passing. Admire them, they are mightier than they look.

EastDulwich www.eastdulwichforum.co.uk

This is a rare breed of phenomenally successful hyperlocal community. At the moment, most hyperlocal communities fail because they don't properly follow the online community development lifecycle.

Element14 http://www.element14.com

If ever there were an organization that just got it right, Element14 would be it—a terrific community of practice from Newark. Also notice the use of symbol as a name here; most communities should do this.

Harringay Online http://www.harringayonline.com

Harringay Online has been growing in importance as a hyperlocal community for some time now. Hugh and the team have done a wonderful job in creating this community and growing many other hyperlocal communities.

IndieTalk www.indietalk.com

A thriving online community of people who discuss independent films. It doesn't have a purpose as such, but it brings together people with a very specific interest.

Lawyers.com http://www.lawyers.com

I'm not quite sure how they secured the domain name, but this really is a terrific online community for those in the law profession. There are many others, but this one still reigns supreme in its field. It also closely fits Etienne Wenger's Community of Practice theory.

Lithium Community Health Index http://pages.lithium.com/community-health-index.html

Despite my gentle knocking of their overly complicated final formula, the Lithium Community Health Index is a fantastic free resource you can use to measure the health of your online community.

MacMillan Cancer http://community.macmillan.org.uk

Not the easiest topic to talk about but certainly one of the most important. Communities of circumstance provide help and support for millions around the world. The people who manage these communities are rock stars. They deal with many of the most extreme emotions in the world. Members pass on, newcomers arrive, fights occur, and medical opinion is debated. Admire the managers of communities of circumstance.

ShootingPeople http://shootingpeople.org

A community of practice. Filmmakers join this community to share advice and advance their expertise in the field.

SK-Gaming http://www.sk-gaming.com

A community for people into competitive video gaming. I've had the pleasure of following this Scandinavian-based community for over a decade now. It's a great example of both web reputation systems in action and ensuring the community is always bustling with activity.

SwordForum http://www.swordforum.com

Like CoinTalk above, but for swords. Do you love swords? Well now you can join a community about them. A terrific example of a successful community.

The Unofficial Greenpeace Community http://planet520.org/forum

Perhaps these guys are a little crazy, but they are solid believers of the cause. Very interesting that some feel that Greenpeace aren't active enough, so they've developed an unofficial community of action. Unofficial communities are more common than you think—especially with non-profits and sports teams.

W14 http://w14london.ning.com

W14 is another thriving hyperlocal community. It's a pity it doesn't have a better name, but it's another good example of a successful community based upon a simple platform.

Recommended Reading

Allan, K.T and Allan, K.H. (1971) Sensitivity training for community leaders, Proceedings of the Annual Convention of the American Psychological Association.

Short extract here, but you can find the more detailed article if you're willing to pay a small fee. It explains the contact hypothesis with a modern twist on Allbrown's original theory.

Arguello, M., Butler, B., Joyce, E., Kraut, R., Ling, K.S., Wang, X. 2006. Talk to me: Foundations for successful individual-group interactions in online communities. ACM Conference on Human-Factors in Computing Systems, New York: ACM Press. 959-96.

Fantastic paper detailing research in converting newcomers into regulars. Highlights importance of newcomers receiving early feedback upon their contributions and the types of early messages newcomers should post that will help them gain feedback.

Aronson, E., & Mills, J. (1959). The effect of severity of initiation on liking for a group. Journal of Abnormal & Social Psychology, 59, 177-181.

A classic article on the effects of hazing and the increased sense of bonding it generates. Worth reading for community processes.

Berge, Z.L. (1995) The Role of the Online Instructor/Facilitator, Education Today, Vol 35.

An early exploration of online facilitation within a teaching context. There are plenty of sound recommendations here for the three roles highlighted by Berge.

Blanchard, Al. and Markus, M.L. (2004) The Experienced "Sense" of a Virtual Community: Characteristics and Practice, The DATA BASE or Advanced Information Systems, Winter 2004.

An update on the work of sense of community using a study of MSN. This study is used as a template for broader generalizations about community management.

Bogart, L. and Orenstein, F.E. (1965) Mass media and community identity in an inter-urban setting, Journalism Quarterly, Vol 42. No. 2. Pp. 179 – 188.

A widely-cited article highlighting the importance of newspapers over television in the development of communities. Only the abstract is available here, academic access to this study will be required to read the full article.

Chalip, L. (2006) Towards Social Leverage of Sports Events, Journal of Sport & Tourism, Vol 11. No. 2. Pp. 109 – 127.

A comprehensive article studying the impact events have upon communities. While specific to sports it's easy to see how this can be broadened to include most events in any context.

Cluett, L. and Seah, H.W.B. (2011) Measuring Success: A case study in evaluating an online community using the Facebook fan pages for UWA students, Teaching and Learning Forum 2011.

While this study does unfortunately use Facebook as an example, it still provides several useful insights into the state of online community management.

Coghlan, M. (2001) eModeration – Managing a New Language, Net*orking 2001 Conference – From Virtual to Reality.

Michael uses very practical examples to guide moderation in key areas and suggests further areas of research. While some of this material is a little dated, much can still be applied. A high focus is on the interpersonal relationships developed with community members.

Collins, M. and Berge, Z. (1996) Facilitation Interaction in Computer Mediated Online Courses, FSU/AECT Distance Education Conference, Tallahasee FL. June.

Demers, D.P., (1996) Does personal experience in a community increase or decrease newspaper reading? Journalism and Mass Communications Quarterly, Vol 73. No. 2. Pp. 304 – 318.

Developing a Sense of Community Measure http://www.psych.uncc.edu/alblanch/BLANCHARDSOVCMeasure.pdf.

Using the material from her previous study, Anita Blanchard tackles the challenge of developing a sense of community again. The model is interesting, but I still prefer the original developed by MacMillan and Chavis.

Dholakia, U.M., Bagozzi, R.P. and Pearo, L.K. (2004) A social influence model of consumer participation in network- and small-group-based virtual communities, International Journal of Research in Marketing, Vol 21. Pp. 241 - 263.

Edelstein, A.S. and Larsen, O.N. (1960) The weekly press' contribution to a sense of urban community, Journalism Quarterly, Vol 37. Pp. 489 – 498.

Finnegan, J.R., Jr and Viswanath, K. (1988) Community ties and use of cable TV and newspapers in a Midwest suburb, Journalism Quarterly, Vol 65. Pp. 456 – 463.

Fredline, L., Deery, M. and Jago, L. (2006) Host Community Perception of the Impacts of Events: A Comparison of Different Event Themes in Urban and Regional Communities.

A detailed and comprehensive study covering the impacts of events upon host communities. Read this if you would like to become more familiar with the topic.

Honeycutt, C. (2005) Hazing as a Process of Boundary Maintenance in an Online Community, Journal of Computer-Mediated Communication, Vol 10. No. 2.

A fascinating review of hazing processes in online communities and their benefits to members of the community.

Janowitz, M. (1952) The community press in our urban setting: The social elements of urbanism.

An aging and hard-to-find book examining the role of local media in establishing a community. While dated from a technical and sociological viewpoint, as most pre-60s books are, its theories are still proven relevant to this day.

Jones, Q., Moldovan, Mihai., Raban, D., and Butler, B. (2008) Empirical evidence of information overload constraining chat channel community interactions. Proceedings of the 2008 ACM conference on computer supported cooperated network.

Jones, Q. Ravid, G. and Rafaeli, S. (2004) Information Overload and the Message Dynamics of Online Interactions Spaces: A Theoretical Model and Empirical Exploration, Information Systems Research, Vol 15. No. 2. Pp. 194 – 210.

One of the few empirically validated articles on information overload within a community. This is a bigger problem than we realize. You should read this article and then give serious thought to how you prevent information overload from occurring.

Lampe, C. and Johnston, E. (2005) Follow the (Slash) dot: Effects of Feedback on New Members in an Online Community, Proceedings of the 2005 international ACM.

A case study of feedback and its different levels in influencing new members to become regular members of the online community.

Lampe, C. and Resnick, P. (2004) Slash(dot) and Burn: Distributed Moderation in a Large Online Space, ACM Computer Human Interaction Conference, 2004.

A fascinating argument for distributed moderation in which a great deal of power is handed to community members. These members then highlight what they feel needs to be removed in the community. This is a good idea. However, it may fall victim to groupthink, bullying and peer pressure. Online community moderation will still be required to prevent this (and perform other essential roles).

Lazar, J. Dr. and Preece, J. Dr. (2002) Social Considerations in Online Communities: Usability, Sociability, and Success Factors, Cognition in the Digital World.

McLeod, J.M., Daily, K., Gui.Z., Everland, W.P. Jr., Bayer, K., Yang, S. and Wang, H. (1996) Community Integration, Local Media Use and Democratic Processes, Communication Research, Vol 23. No. 2. pp. 179 – 209.

An excellent study that both thoroughly reviews existing theories concerning community integration and local media and studies its impacts with regards to psychological attachment, interpersonal discussion networks and whether individuals have a connection to their local or broader communities.

Owen, J.E., Bantum, E.O'C., Golant, M. (2008) Benefits and challenges experienced by professional facilitators of online support groups for cancer survivors, Psycho-Oncology.

An excellent study in facilitation of online groups within a health context. While the context will distort the ability to generalize from these results, there is still plenty of provocative material here in the tasks undertaken by online facilitators and the obstacles they face.

Preece, J. (2004) Etiquette Online: From nice to necessary, Communications of the ACM.

Ren, Y and Kraut, R.E. (2008) Simulating Newcomer Socialization in Online Communities, Working paper.

A short read about the different theories involved in converting newcomers into regular members of the community. It informed much of the background material for this book.

Ridings, C.M. and Gefen, D. (2004) Virtual Community Attraction: Why People Hang Out Online, Journal for Computer Mediated Communication, Vol 10, No. 1.

An interesting review of the motivations behind participation in a community and how to sustain interest in a community over a period of time.

Sangwan, S. (2005) Virtual Community Success: a Uses and Gratifications Perspective, Proceedings of the 38th Hawaii International Conference on System Sciences.

An often-cited study to ascertain the uses and gratifications of an online community. This is most relevant for how to offer newcomers something that will interest them enough to participate.

Sense of Community: A Definition and Theory (1986).

McMillan and Chavis' groundbreaking original work explaining the psychological sense of community people within a community have with one another. This plays a crucial role in understanding what communities need.

Souza, C.S.d., and Preece, J. (2004) A framework for analyzing and understanding online communities, Interacting with Computers, Vol 16. Pp. 579 – 610.

Stamm, K.R., and Fortini-Campbell, L., (1983) The relationship of community ties to newspaper use, Association for Education if Journalism and Mass Communications, Vol 84. Pp 27.

Testing a model of sense of community http://www.psych.uncc.edu/alblanch/TestingaModelCIHB.pdf.

An important article by Anita Blanchard who tackles whether online communities have the same sense of community as offline communities.

Tewkesbury, D. (2006) What Do Americans Really Want To Know? Tracking the Behaviors of News Readers On The Internet, Journal of Communication, Vol 53. No. 4. Pp. 694 – 710.

Wertz, C. and Ruyter, K.d., (200x) Beyond the Call of Duty: Why Customers Contribute to Firm-hosted Commercial Online Communities, Organizational Studies, Vol 28, No 3. Pp. 347 – 376.

Williams, R.L. and Cothrel, J. (2000) Four Smart Ways To Run Online Communities, Sloan Management Review, Summer, 2000.

Young, B., Ceullar, M.J., and Takeda, H. (2011) Investigating the Impact of Offline Events on Group Development in an Online Sports Community, Proceedings of the Southern Association for Information Systems Conference, 2011.

This is one of the best studies undertaken thus far detailing how offline events affect an online community. It also includes an excellent literature review of existing material on this topic.

About The Author

Richard Millington is the founder and managing director of FeverBee Limited, a community consultancy dedicated to improving how organizations develop communities. He is also the founder of The Pillar Summit, the world's first and most comprehensive course in Professional Community Management.

Richard has worked on dozens of successful community projects, and his client list is one of the most impressive in the industry. Clients include The United Nations, Oracle, The Global Fund, BAE Systems, AMD, OECD, The RSPCA, Future Publishing, The British Medical Journal, EMC and a variety of youth and entertainment brands.

Richard's blog, www.feverbee.com, is widely cited for introducing best practices in developing communities.

Contact Richard@feverbee.com or +44 (0)20 7792 2469.

About The Pillar Summit

The Pillar Summit is an intensive community management course for Professional Community Managers. The goal of the course is to supply students with all the skills, knowledge, and resources they need to become world-class community managers.

It is the first course dedicated to training community managers to build and manage communities for brands. The Pillar Summit Alumni include community managers from Lego, Greenpeace, Amazon, Oracle, PatientsLikeMe, and Telligent.

The Pillar Summit brings proven academic theory, practical tactics and solid standards to the world of community management. It provides participants with a solid framework for developing and sustaining a thriving online community.

You can sign up for The Pillar Summit at: www.pillarsummit.com.

48593622R00164

Made in the USA
San Bernardino, CA
17 August 2019